Games Grandmas Play

D1444046

Games Grandmas Play

Life Lessons on
Christian Faith and Grandchildren

Joan Jacobs

Illustrations by Carol Cuatt

Geneva Press
Louisville, Kentucky

Scripture quotations from the New Revised Standard Version of the Bible are copyright © 1989 by the Division of Christian Education of the National Council of the Churches of Christ in the U.S.A. and are used by permission.

Excerpt from Medema, Ken, "Color Outside the Lines," © 1996 Brier Patch Music. Reprinted by permission. Excerpt from Marsh, Charles, *God's Long Summer,* © 1997 Princeton University Press. Reprinted by per-mission of Princeton University Press.

Book design by Sharon Adams
Book illustrations by Carol Cuatt
Cover design by Night and Day Design

First edition
Published by Geneva Press
Louisville, Kentucky

This book is printed on acid-free paper that meets the American National Standards Institute Z39.48 standard. ♾

PRINTED IN THE UNITED STATES OF AMERICA

01 02 03 04 05 06 07 08 09 10 — 10 9 8 7 6 5 4 3 2 1

Library of Congress Cataloging-in-Publication Data

Jacobs, Joan, 1925–
    Games grandmas play: life lessons on Christian faith and grand-children / Joan Jacobs. — 1st ed.
        p. cm.
    Includes bibliographical references.
    ISBN 0-664-50150-8 (alk. paper)
    1. Grandmothers—Religious life. 2. Grandparent and child—Religious aspects—Christianity. 3. Games—Religious aspects—Christianity. I. Title.

BV4847 .J33 2001
248.8'45—dc21   00-062286

To some special people:
the parents of my grandchildren
and my extended family

CONTENTS

ACKNOWLEDGMENTS

I have received and welcomed lots of support, ideas, and encouragement. John McClure (having instructed me how to e-mail whole chapters) faithfully read and edited, Annie McClure made some valuable suggestions, Sally MacLeod and Chris Freeman (wise and active grandmothers) read and commented. Shelley Jacobs rescued me from computer glitches. Marie Cardwell and Helen Brown (other grandmothers), Darlane Jespersen, Laurie Simon, and Honey Chambers, having sampled and approved, prayed for me and the book for many months. Two people (both grandparents) read the manuscript uncritically and enjoyed it, of course an encouragement: Dee Engel, Minister to Children and Families at Trinity United Presbyterian Church of Santa Ana, California, and Dr. James Laughrun, a psychoanalyst in practice in Pasadena, California. All of these people were a great boost. Of course I am grateful to Geneva Press and my editor, Martha Gilliss, for their acceptance, expertise, and on-going guidance. I also offer grateful thanks for steady support from my immediate and extended families whenever the book was a subject of conversation.

The music of Ken Medema has enriched me over many years, and I am grateful to him and Brier Patch Music for permission to quote the chorus of "Color Outside the Lines" in the chapter of this book, "Coloring: Living Inside and Outside Expectations."

READY, GET SET, GO

(Beginning to Play)

Games are fun—if they aren't there's not much point in playing. Some of the games I've enjoyed with my grandchildren are the chapter titles of this book. I have five married children, and in these last months and years I've spent considerable time with each family and have been called Grandma or Grammie more often than my given name. My name is Grandma.

My son-in-law suggested I write about being a Christian grandmother, and I immediately remembered the discomfort Madeleine L'Engle felt when asked to address a group about being a Christian writer. Later she wrote, "To try to talk about art and about Christianity is for me one and the

1

same thing . . ."¹ I find it true that talking about being a grandmother and a Christian is one subject. Long before I became a grandmother I worked at the integration of my self with my faith and there's no doubt that this work has had its effect on my grandparenting.

The oldest of my grandchildren, Ian and Leslie, are teenagers whose parents wondered if they'd ever have cousins. Then a few years ago the cousins began to arrive. In order of their appearance, C. J. (short for Christopher John) came five years after Leslie was born, and then Andrew, Deanna, Madison, Casey and Steven (who could almost be twins except they have different parents), and finally Matthew. Each family has a son and a daughter, except one: Andrew has special brothers, his first cousins Victor, Josúe, and another Matthew, who have come to be like grandsons to me.

The only consistent commonality among grandmothers is grandchildren. So much depends on circumstances: distance, physical well-being, family attitudes, what life has been like in the past, what it's like now. There is amazing diversity among us. It seems that not every grandma is happy with this particular designation. One woman told me that under no condition would she "baby-sit." On the other hand, one grandmother I know is raising two grandsons, another is raising six.² Many grandparents are now sharing their home with a single-parent son or daughter who has come back bringing children. Many grandmothers lie incapacitated in nursing homes. This summer I met a beautiful young woman with a two-year-old in tow—she was the grandmother! Some grandmothers are in the work force and haven't much time or energy for the grandchildren they love. Great-aunts and older friends or neighbors are often surrogates who have assumed the role of grandparent, as in my relationship with Andrew's cousins. While grandma-descriptions seem limitless, in this book I'm thinking about those grandmothers who want to be and are free to be in a relatively close relationship to their grandchildren.

Sometimes this diversity among grandmothers arises from the way we are received in our children's homes. For a long time I've known that some parents of grown children, especially mothers, aren't genuinely welcome. Over the years relationships have somehow fallen apart. I recall the sympathy offered by our son-in-law's friend when he heard that I was arriving for a three-week visit, and the chagrin of another on learning of my arrival to help our daughter celebrate her fortieth birthday. One grandmother whose pain was visible showed me little-girl pictures of her twelve-year-old granddaughter whose parents had mutually decided to eliminate both sets of grandparents from their lives; she did not know why.

Grandfathers are not left out of this book because they aren't important. Even our little ones reflected on Grandpa a long time after he was gone. When I take Madison, who lives near me, to the playground, grandpas are sometimes there. While it seems that grandpas are increasingly present in their grandchildren's lives, perhaps grandmothers are the more involved now because in past generations mothers had the greatest parenting role. It's a new thing, in general, for fathers to take the active role I see in my own children's families—as grandfathers these men will shine!

More than one person has said to me, "Enjoy your grandchildren while they're little. Teenagers won't have much time for you." Apart from the fact that our family teenagers live halfway across the country, that statement is generally true. Life gets far more complicated in the teen years. Energies are demanded and absorbed increasingly outside the home (where grandmas on visits are likely to hang out). We grandmas can provide some solid background stability, but the only games I seem to be able to play with my teenager grandchildren is to watch and cheer from the grandstands at sports events, attend an awards assembly or a school play, or enjoy an occasional board game.

In choosing to center my thinking around games that fit childhood, I realize that sometimes adult talk about playing games is a cover for something else, a way to deceive: "He's just playing games with her" or "She's still playing games, maybe she can't be real." The games I'm thinking about are the ways children actually play. For children the fun of games is serious business: a child's play is a child's work.

Children's games often lend themselves to worthwhile reflection on the far larger game of life. The games I've chosen as chapter subjects suggest ways grandmas can encourage grandchildren as they grow up, and they point to some strategies for living we ourselves can find useful. I have divided each chapter into three categories: a description of the game, how the game plays out with grandchildren, and how the game lends itself to ideas for our own personal enrichment. These categories turned out to be uneven within the chapters—some games seemed to fit better in one than another. In each chapter, in the personal enrichment category, I have separated the term "herself" to read "her self" to emphasize that our personal growth takes place with the intimate inner self we so often neglect.

Children have no need to make these adult connections between their games and life; it is enough if a child grows up with pleasant memories of playing with parents and grandparents. The give and take of games—winning and losing, playing fair and finishing well—is good preparation for the years to come.

Games would lose purpose without rules, and there are

guidelines for grandmothering that help to define our role. Grandmothers usually have a strong set of principles that they bring to the game of life and we are sometimes tempted to pass them on, to try changing things in the homes of grown children. Our adult children began their run for independence in their teens and arrived there years ago. When as adults our children establish their own households, two traditions meet. It would stifle God's creativity if the result were a mirror image of either home in which one was raised. My daughters don't fold their towels the way I do and my sons before marrying had no idea they were folded by anybody.

The influence of the home of one's childhood is inescapable when raising children, for good or ill, but it is not our job in our grandmothering years to bring that past to the present. The benefit of age and experience should play out behind the scenes in more imaginative ways. A wise grandma learns to spend time with grandchildren honoring the standards developed by their moms and dads and in tune with the general atmosphere of each family. I am not, for instance, the TV rule-maker regardless of how I feel about it (though undoubtedly my likes and dislikes get communicated!).

When I'm in charge of grandchildren I take direction gladly. For instance, I've needed to be reeducated about safety rules and if sometimes the instruction is unnecessary I take it anyway. I find scarcely any cause for the wisdom of age to apply here since I'm occasionally careless. I simply remind myself that as a grandmother I keep learning. On a recent visit to grandchildren I left the driveway gate ajar and my daughter-in-law quickly shut it, remarking: "This is my worst nightmare." Their dog was sitting close by and I thought, "Well, he doesn't want to go anywhere." Then the dawn broke that she was referring, of course, to their two-year-old!

Abuse does happen in families regardless of economic status. If a grandmother knows that abuse of children or a parent is taking place, the rule of non-interference goes, of course, out the window. No one should stand by when there is a need to speak out and confront abusive behavior, or to call the police.

If you're an old hand with your younger families you've probably worked out some guidelines for yourself. Each of us comes from a different place and we approach our families in different ways. God accepts us where we are and knows our circumstances. None of our households is a duplicate of another. We and our families are unique, and grandmas have the challenge of filling the role each in her own special way. Fresh or renewed wisdom is often called for as we work our way in the grandmothering business. "If any of you is lacking in wisdom," the Bible tells us, "ask God, who gives to all generously and ungrudgingly, and it will be given you." (James 1:5)

My own experiences are reflected here, and occasionally I manipulated the present. I asked C. J. to play SORRY with me so I could refresh myself about the game for that chapter. Sometimes I found myself musing over some recent event: would it contribute to the text? In any event, it all happened.

We grandmothers will serve ourselves well if we can keep a light hand, a sense of adventure, on each shared experience with grandchildren, even when those experiences are somewhat strained or stressful. Even when we have major responsibilities with our grandchildren the idea of games will help us to create the space, the perspective we need for our own lives. Let our games begin!

Notes

1. Madeleine L'Engle, *Walking On Water: Reflections on Faith and Art* (New York: Bantam, 1982), 16.

2. "A Census Bureau report indicates that 3.9 million children are living in homes maintained by their grandparents." *Parade Magazine, 26* March 2000. The American Association of Retired Persons' Grandparent Information Center addresses legal, social, health, and financial issues faced by grandparents. Write to the American Association of Retired Persons GIC, Dept. P, 601 E St., N.W., Washington, D.C. 20049, or e-mail gic@aarp.org or visit www.aarp.org/w.,confacts/programs/ gic.html on the Web.

One

HIDE AND SEEK

(Listening and Being Found)

The Game

Hide and Seek is a flexible game with little ones and can be played anywhere—a park, a playground, at home. This is true because there's no need to really hide—a skinny tree, the back of a slide, a chair—all work for them. They think that if their eyes are closed or covered they're invisible.

There's more than one way to play. Madison, when nearly three, hid her face, counted "One, two, three, four," but frowned and objected when I slipped away. She wanted to count *and* hide. Well-played, one sneaks quietly to the best hiding place possible and hopes not to be found, but none of my grands, at least before the age of five, can bear to be hidden very long. A hint will soon come—a whisper, a cough, some small sound, and I follow the sound to its source because even feeling hidden is a bit scary and being found is so exciting.

Grandmas and Grandchildren

Grandmas can play the roles both of "listener" and "finder" in the lives of our grandchildren. Hearing where they are coming from is challenging as well as interesting. We are privileged listeners to the sounds that can clue us in to whatever is going on in their lives. Hide and Seek turns out to be part of a serious game.

Grownups sometimes consider listening to a child either too difficult, too boring, or too indulgent. Adults are often not willing to spend the energy it takes to listen. This is one of the gaps that grandparents can fill in the lives of their grandchildren: attentive listening by a significant adult. When any of us is really heard our worth is affirmed. The old adage "Children should be seen and not heard" is not a wise saying and it was not true for me as a child. I cannot remember having had to be continually silent at home in order to guarantee peace for grown-ups, and neither have my grandchildren. If a grandma isn't willing to listen, it may be because over the years she has not been listened to and granted that gift.

Listening to our grandchildren can happen in several ways. Body language speaks loudly if we are watching. Tears are so obvious that we may miss other more subtle sounds. I could tell from the thrust of his shoulders as he mounted his front steps that one little friend was angry. Facial expressions give away the feelings of a child. Two of my grandchildren get a sparkle of mischief in their eyes and it's a challenge to "listen" for what comes next! The sober silent withdrawal of a child from the current scene is a signal that all isn't well. The stubborn refusal to do something is more than a signal of obstinacy—there's a reason that needs to be heard.

A combination of verbal and body language is telling. Who knows, until you rush to find out, what a scream means? One of our two-year-olds gets red in the face and her voice rises as I have failed to understand her for the third or fourth time and, concerned, I finally remember to ask, "Can you show me?" The bright-eyed interest of our eight-year-old was pure pleasure as he described how close the bald eagle came to losing to the wild turkey its place as our American symbol.

Eye contact helps in listening and hearing. Pictures in an old Life magazine showed the world as it looks from the perspective of a small child—table legs, chair legs, human legs—dull, unresponsive uprights. In the comic strip "For Better or Worse," grownups at an airport are happily greeting each other and April, the child, standing waist high, thinks, "Some day, when I'm big, I'm going to remember to talk to short people." In the comic "Jump Start" the little children refer to us as "the giants." When a giant stoops to make eye contact it's very impressive, whether the eye is communicating kindness or disapproval. It's at least a courtesy to get low enough to speak to the eyes. I resort to a chair, and when I need to talk the child seems willing enough to meet me there.

Grandma's eye contact can itself be a problem-solver because a child knows he's been heard. Not long ago Andrew and Josúe were tearing around the backyard on trikes when one blocked the other and got a mild punch in the back as reward. His feelings were more hurt than his body. Once seated I caught his eye, beckoned him over, rubbed the spot, remonstrated with the other offender, and that was it. Had feelings not been heard the event could have turned into a major sulk and required far more energy to placate.

Does a grandma have the time and patience to hear? Not always, and a lapse is an effective teacher. Recently in a family crisis involving an accident and a rush to the emergency room, I was the caregiver at home and our three-year-old grew increasingly wakeful and upset as the evening wore on. Admonitions to stay in bed met with increasing resistance and finally tears. Impatience was looming and "Sweetie, stop crying" didn't work. I wasn't really listening as I put my own concern about the accident in front of her welfare. Finally with big brother's cuddling, and some music, sleep came. The next morning as I recalled the scene the night before, her mother reminded me of another way to listen that I certainly knew but had failed to practice. Reflective listening works: variations on "I know you're upset" and "It feels bad when Mommy and Daddy aren't home" would have resolved our tensions much sooner. Reflective listening, the art of "hearing" where a child is coming from and letting her know you hear, is a skill easily intellectualized and needs airing in practice.

To be heard is important, but as children get a little older they also discover that they like secrets, that they can hide something inside. The desire of parents to control for the sake of a child's well-being (and plain curiosity) causes them to ask lots of questions when a child is old enough to have some secrets of his own. Grandmas might have the same temptation. Paul Tournier, who gave us enormous insight into becoming whole persons, wrote about secrets:

> The prestige of a secret is very great in the mind of the child. . . . To know something which others do not, is to become a person, distinct from other persons . . . A

child's secrets must be respected. Something vitally important is at stake: nothing less than the formation of his person.[1]

Dr. Tournier goes on to say that the child also wants to be free to tell a secret, not only to demonstrate that she really has one, but to prove "the free disposition of oneself:"[2] I can have a secret, I can tell it, I am my own person! Unfortunately when something is withheld and parental pressure is very firm and perhaps somewhat scary, the ground is ripe for lies. When caring adults have been consistently kind and understanding, opening up is easier when the pressure is off; children do try to please.

Sensitivity is necessary with another kind of secret: the talk between grandparent and mom or dad about a child's behavior can set up barriers between adults and children. When something said or done has strayed from what we find appropriate, do we tell the parents? Maybe, but some time ago I said to C. J., who was then seven, "I won't talk to your mother or dad about anything unless I've talked to you first." The occasion for this escapes me—it was something minor or I was just setting ground rules—but it struck me as important in keeping communication clear.

A mom noticed a small impudence toward me on a grandchild's part and asked me about it. I had noticed it at the time, and now appreciated two things: that attention had been drawn to it so we could put it behind us, and that it's the most natural thing in the world for a child to try out something new, to imitate something heard at school or simply experiment with a new idea. If I had called her on it right away I could have said to her mom, "We have already talked about this." It's a compliment to parents or a grandma when they get to hear the new thing—a child senses when acceptance and firm kindness rule. Children may also want to hide feelings they think would be poorly received, a natural defense against perceived, and perhaps real, disapproval or threat: not liking food at a hostess' table, jealousy over a toy, a gift that doesn't please. This is a different kind of secret, but also a reassurance that he can be a person separate from the parents. One cannot deny a reasonableness in such hiding if negative feelings have been verbally judged as bad. Grandmas may or may not sense when something is being withheld, but our relationship isn't colored by this hiding—it is not our business.

Grandmas have no need to pry. We can be the safe place where everything is all right, where it's okay to have a secret because we are not giving way to curiosity. Questions have a role to play in our conduct with grandchildren, but not for the sake of intrusion into their privacy. I once asked a psychotherapist for some advice about one of our children and after some hesitation (therapists being thin on advice!) he said, "Don't ask." "Don't ask" works with family adults as well. We are bound by our love and caring to be interested and curious about what is going on in their lives, but not asking invasive questions leaves them with their adulthood and leaves us the space we need for separateness.

Accepting our grandchildren where they are gives them a sense of security free from the worry that we are trying to impose ourselves on them. If we are actually in charge, the scene changes when something comes up and disclosure is necessary; a "secret" may begin to tell itself on a guilty face, but that is a different kind of secret.

This place of the secure and unquestioning grandma is important with teen-agers. There is a child within our teenagers, a child we remember vividly and a child they are trying to leave behind. They know they are children no longer and are now struggling to become independent. They want to relate to us as adults, even though the time is not quite ripe.

My teenaged grandchildren have always lived far away; en route to their home for visits I had some concern about reentry into their lives. Would we get along well? We always have, but I am frankly somewhat at sea with the teen years. I respect the enormous and rapid changes taking place inside them and in their relationships at home, school, church, and especially with their peers. I remember their need to be trusted and the integrity that comes with trust, and yet life presents them with highly charged choices that need parameters from responsible adults. I do not really understand the world they are swiftly entering and find myself glad to defer to parents. Teenagers especially need to have secrets; would I want to know what they are? Prayerful listening, without prying, opens up a space between us that allows normal conversations, even though often centered on themselves and their interests.

Grandma Her Self

Like children, we grandmas also need to be heard. Over the years we have developed patterns of listening to others and to ourselves. Listening to yourself is important. Like anyone else, grandmas can have personal secrets, but there is a kind of secret, a way of hiding, that is not healthy. A painful past can hide within if you have not consciously worked through it. We each have a large place for storage in our minds where unhandled painful events stay alive in our unconsciousness. If you are hiding behind what has hurt you, it means that at some level you have not been heard.

As grandmothers, this hiding is significant because guarding a painful interior part of us takes energy, and it is energy stolen from the present. When strength is used to keep pain hidden you may not have the will or the resources for grandchildren. To be open and free in spirit you have to come to terms with whatever is bottled up inside.

Plenty of grandmas have been open to themselves since childhood, painful experiences accepted for what they were and worked through, that is, the pain was felt and consciously lived with. When that happened, nothing painful was stored inside and negative memories mercifully faded—though traumatic events may not be forgotten, the feelings connected with them are diminished or no longer felt. As children, these grandmas did not need to hide for the sake of pleasing or sparing the adults in their lives; they had the freedom or courage to express and to process troubling things when they happened.

Many of us did not have that freedom over the years—when traumatic things happened the negative feelings that should have been worked through were instead ignored, pushed away, and finally became walls that forced our real selves into hiding. We were not heard, and we hid experiences that hurt.

Later in life it's not always easy to find another human being to hear us, someone with whom we are willing to unveil trouble from the past that still holds us down in the present. Sadly, many women and men in my generation have found churches to be of little value in hearing us where we are. God does not hear us from some distant somewhere in the sky. God hears us but works for us through the caring ears of one another. It is my hope that churches everywhere will learn to be for grandmas what grandmas can be for their grandchildren: listeners who attend with acceptance and love to the signals that come from behind life's walls. God never intended us to go it alone. God is vitally concerned that we should be in mutually listening relationships with other people. God is God and can meet us in many mysterious ways, but one proven way is in the warmth of an accepting person or group.

If you would like to share troublesome unresolved things with someone, begin by asking God for the right person or persons. A next step might be journaling. I have friends for whom a journal serves as a confidant and silently receives one's most distressing past; sometimes writing it down provides the needed relief. If you have asked God for someone, or a group of people with whom you can be honest about where and who you are, take your time and be on the lookout for God's answer. Sometimes simply because we have made a definite request to God for help a hope glimmers, and hope allows us to look around with new eyes and perhaps some measure of peace.

If you are worshiping with a congregation, your church may have a network of counseling opportunities and they are worth looking into. Perhaps a pastor may be of help, but you will have to listen for a pastor who is kind, wise, and not judgmental—a few sermons will tell you this. Perhaps a professional psychotherapist or a psychoanalyst will be your avenue to insight and healing, as both were for me. Perhaps there is a kind and wise woman in the congregation you have overlooked, perhaps someone you have noticed but forgotten about.

There are cautions as you seek help. You can, in a sense, test people by being around them awhile before you decide to talk about yourself:

- Look for someone whose own problems are not consuming her; such a person may be easy to talk to, but you'll get her load and find yours has not become lighter.
- Avoid sharing with someone for whom life seems to be one big rosy glow; such a person may have trouble handling your difficult experiences and the negative feelings that go with them.

- Steer clear of someone who is preachy; such a person gives quick answers that may sound spiritually correct but when tried don't work.
- If you decide to take the courageous step of consulting a professional therapist, get a recommendation from someone you trust.
- Avoid persons whose intent is clearly to indoctrinate, to beckon you into a group that is isolated from other people. Sometimes we are so lonely we can be swept up by cultic ideas and goals.

God always desires to hear us into healing, to listen to our lives—the painful memories, the lost opportunities, the regrets. God uses caring people to bring us to this good place.

Listening and being found are good guides for a grandma. We listen to grandchildren, find the persons they are, and find our place in their lives. We listen to ourselves with acceptance, and seek to understand where and who we are. And we seek others whose listening presence in our lives can hear us into wholeness.

Notes
1. Paul Tournier, *The Meaning of Persons* (New York: Harper & Row, 1957), 125–126.
2. Ibid.

Two

THE PLAYGROUND

(Making Choices)

The Game

Playgrounds are rich places for fun. When a child enters a playground the whole world is, for the moment, before her. The beauty of most playgrounds is their sturdy simplicity—swings, slides and a few assorted ways to climb to them, perhaps a flexible little bridge to tie things together, bars to negotiate or dangle from, sometimes a life-sized animal shape to sit on, and variations on all this.

The value of a playground is hard to overstate. Even if they have been constructed with a particular age group in mind, there is usually something for every child at some

level. The atmosphere is heady with choices. There's freedom to choose. Apart from the warning that in five minutes it will be time to go home, no one is required to do
any one thing for only so long. A child can discover what
he or she likes most to do; different pieces of equipment
call for different skills. All this while expending lots of
energy—one can practically see muscles growing. A
responsible adult is on hand simply of necessity and
because the playground is mildly precarious. An unac-
companied child is immediate cause for concern.

The values multiply. For most children a playground is
a happy place for firsts: the first time to sit in something
that travels back and forth gently through the air, the first
time to climb a ladder, the first time to slide down on
something with waiting arms at the other end, the first
time to negotiate uncertain steps on a wiggly bridge. A
playground is ideal for developing social skills. A child
meets new children, learns to take turns, shares the toys
one has brought (if one so desires) or asks permission to
use the toys of someone else (if the someone wants to
share). A child learns quickly enough who's willing to play
and who isn't. I've watched Madison approach one child
or another in friendly fashion to be received or rejected. A
reception is an occasion for delight—sharing equipment,
running together, sitting under a slide and talking. The
child in me is evoked by such small joys.

Children's personalities are in evidence here. Andrew,
Deanna, Madison, and now Steven and Casey are
attracted to swings. Soaring high appeals to some more
than others—wind in the face, the surges high and low.
One wishes for a high bench for grandmothers to sit on
while pushing. Leslie, at ten having passed her own enthusiasm about swinging, developed a major climbing
craze—perhaps presaging her own aptitude for moving on
to new things. Ignoring the swings (and these were high

ones for older children), she would climb to the very top of the apparatus and slither down the slanty poles. I could only hold my breath.

Sitting at ease on a bench to nurse a cup of coffee is a hope delayed. I've learned to manage a swing with one hand, which is an accomplishment when the swing is at its apex and the call comes to stop. There are occasional moments when a grandma has time to let thoughts run or to talk to some other child-care person.

The playground is the place where children experience the freedom to constantly rechoose what to play next. Climbing and sliding give way to that interest in the toys someone else has brought, while I remember we've forgotten to bring ours! "Watch me!" demands attention and acknowledgment and keeps a grandma on her toes. One watches, at many playgrounds, for flying sand or gravel.

Grandmas and Grandchildren

The playground is not the only place for decision-making and grandmas can be alert to other times when a choice can be made. The kinds of choices grandmas offer most often don't need parental permission. With the guideline in place regarding respect for the parents, we do not offer choices that would violate the trust they place in us.

There is a role for questions here: they can strengthen choice-making and serve us well at the same time. Of course questions can be used to accuse and condemn or to pry, and there are times when they necessarily point to an oversight: "Could you have left your jacket at school? When did you last have it on?" Used by a caring grandma, questions can suggest personal worth, shift appropriate power to a child, relieve tension, demonstrate adult flexibility, and often in the process avoid the trouble of insisting on a particular way to get something done. A nap is rejected: "There's time for one story. Would you rather read it in bed or out here on the couch?" Shoes do not want to go on: "Do you want to put them on or do you want me to?" Doing hair is resisted: "Do you want me to use a brush or a comb, and where would you like to sit?" Apart from the sheer usefulness of it, this simple level of choice-making is nevertheless an exercise in developing the skill.

There's more substance to choices like these: "Which book would you like to read?" "It's a nice day; would you like to go to the park?" "I would like to take a walk; what would you like to do?" Madison and I have entered into a choice regarding TV. I consult the daily TV listings and read off the acceptable choices for the time allotted; she enters into this seriously, and often has me repeat them. This may help differentiate between watching certain programs and just looking at TV. Some choices may call for negotiation, such as the use of time after school: I might ask C. J., "What is your plan for the rest of the afternoon and when does homework fit in?" I can see that beyond the middle of grade school, grandmas probably have less and less to say about the choices a child makes unless it's something like deciding which new good movie to see.

A willingness to allow questions to be a kind of conversational life-style with children (or adults!) helps in developing relationships: one chooses how to answer with a sense of integrity. Since questions can be rude and invasive, asking useful ones becomes an art. Not long ago someone was asking me appropriate questions about my own situation and I thought, "This person really cares about me," while another pushed so many pointed queries I felt myself backing away.

Jesus serves as a model in question-asking; he asked questions, and often answered questions put to him with more of his own. He affirmed personal worth because his questions invited people to think and kept conversations directed and meaningful. Our grandchildren, too, will be affirmed by the kinds of questions that give them choices. The playground freedom to choose is a valuable asset early in life.

Children today generally have more freedom to make choices about food, clothes, and play than we were given as children or than we gave our own—there is certainly more of all these things to choose from. Because many of us were not given the privilege of choices as children we are in a place to learn how important early choice-making is in preparation for major choices in the future. Choosing well, like listening well, is a skill to be learned.

Grandma Her Self

The playground freedom to choose is undergirded by the safety a caring adult provides, and that's a way you as a grandmother can look at your own life. You are given the freedom to make choices and you do so in the warmth of God's care. In his letter to the Christians at Philippi, Paul makes a suggestion appropriate to making our way in the Christian life:

> Work out your own salvation with fear and trembling; for it is God who is at work in you, enabling you both to will and to work for his good pleasure. (Philippians 2:12b-13)

Like the swing at its apex, we are flying and undergirded at the same time. We are affirmed by God's willingness for us to exercise our own judgments and to make our own decisions, and we are cautioned not to be careless because it is God who is at work within us.

The major decision we make as grandmothers is whether or not to be committed to our grandchildren no matter what happens on the playground of life. A decision *for* this commitment is part of how we manifest God's unconditional commitment to us, as expressed so powerfully in the life, death, and rising of Christ. J. Phillip Newell writes:

> The decision to be committed, which is a response to the gift of love, is freely chosen. Once it is made, however, there is the discipline of love, the being committed when we do not necessarily feel like it.[1]

Newell was thinking about the grace of commitment in the middle years not only to marriage and family but to the wider world; I narrow it here to the role of grandparent. Like all commitments, this one to grandchildren needs renewing, and sometimes revising; the commitment doesn't go away, but the store of energy varies.

There's no question that commitment will involve pain: at the very least we become aware of the erosion of our own energies, that at some point we have to be less active with grandchildren. But some grandparents face immediate pain when something devastating happens to a grandchild, and then choice presents itself again. It seems clear that the choice would be to stand as sturdy moral support, whatever our physical energies dictate; for those who make this decision it is nearly unnecessary to mention it. But grandparents can shut down in the face of a tragedy. The six-month-old daughter of friends of one of my families has been diagnosed with a swiftly-moving degenerative syndrome and difficult choices needed to be made regarding critical and invasive medical treatment. One set of grandparents has been very restrained in coming alongside.

Choosing commitment in the face of tragedy is clearly demonstrated by Jesus himself, and the closer he came to the place of his death the more consciously he carried his decision to do God's will, to do what he knew had to be done, to go where he had to go. He had turned toward

Jerusalem for the last time, knowing he would die there, and we read, "He went on his way through towns and villages, teaching, and journeying to Jerusalem . . ." After speaking with some Pharisees, he said, "Yet today, tomorrow, and the next day I must be on my way." (Luke 13:33). We feel with him: He takes one day at a time. He is not dragging his feet, but it is heavy going. I find comfort and challenge in this commitment of Jesus, who chose over and over again to be committed to this world in which there is so much sin, evil, and suffering. Any uncertainty or lack of purpose of my own, or occasional weariness, is challenged by Christ's companionship.

A decision basic to one's activity as a grandmother is the care of one's self, thereby relieving our families of the need to dote or nag. At several points it has seemed that my body was determined to undermine me in one way or another. I'm not a hypochondriac—this is just what happens as the years roll on.

Weight is an important consideration—too much is a hazard: hard on the heart and joints. We are old and wise enough to know we weren't born that way. Usually it isn't in the genes; one's metabolic rate may be a hindrance but we are responsible for the pounds. Weight certainly determines some aspects of our role as grandmas. After many attempts with different systems, Weight Watchers worked for me—I needed some accountability in this area. Self-control, that wonderful attribute of the spirit, is always the key and if one is a food lover the challenge is big. Food—with its marvelous comforting quality!

There is a bewildering array of conditions that can affect our bodies, many of them *not* chosen. Osteoarthritis is a scourge that comes on with aging—first this joint or that one. The Arthritis Foundation has chapters in every state and major city with toll-free numbers and furnishes a great deal of helpful information and support. Our hearts play tricks on us as they develop weaknesses and there seems to be no end of advice about this. We can choose to take the best possible physical care of our bodies, realizing that a positive approach to life plays an important part in our overall health. We want to stay on the playground as long as possible!

Our choosing has its lighter side: to stay in touch with people we enjoy and to take the initiative in doing that; to spend time with other Christians learning, thinking, and worshiping in a satisfying congregation or group; to make efforts to insure that we have what we need for rewarding leisure time.

The woman who furnished me with information about the Arthritis Foundation is a volunteer grandmother. One grandma is happily welcomed into grade school classrooms once a week for story-reading, one tutors at the local Boys and Girls Club, one shares a morning a week with a seriously ill shut-in, one spends time in a common-sense center where young women find help in avoiding abortion. If grandchildren are at a distance or don't absorb all the time you find available, there is an additional place for your energy, a place where your compassion can be used. Every local church congregation has built-in opportunities for the exercise of every ability we have. Even a little time is appreciated by people who need help. Volunteers not only enrich our world, they make richer grandparents.

We can look at the playground as a place for the freedom to make choices. A gift to our grandchildren is to create a safe space for the freedom they need in learning how to choose well. For our part, healthy options come to us in the aging process, and we need to exercise them in the freedom God gives.

Notes

1. J. Philip Newell, *One Foot in Eden* (Mahwah, N.J.: Paulist Press, 1999), 63.

Three

PUZZLES

(Working Through It)

The Game

Puzzles intrigue all of us, children and adults. Four-year-old Deanna asked me to help with her jigsaw, large pieces featuring Donald, Daisy, Minnie, Mickey, and Pluto. She was, I thought, extraordinarily clever in matching colors and shapes. She added a piece.

"Good for you," I said, and handed her another one.

"But I can do it myself."

"I thought you wanted me to help."

She fitted the piece and worked on. When the temptation overcame me to add one, she said, "Good for you, Grammie; you did it."

Some puzzle-toys for toddlers are simple shapes with handles to fit into matching spaces. I once worked with pieces of a small wooden train track with lots of options; one set of tracks was intended only for a figure eight, but toddler-like, I spent quite a while trying to make one big circle of it. One jigsaw was a six-foot jungle scene to be assembled on the floor. On family vacations we often set up an elaborate jigsaw. Life furnishes more sobering kinds of puzzles that come and go or stick with us over the years.

Grandmas and Grandchildren

A simple but effective way for grandmas to help children develop problem-solving abilities is to begin with the provision of puzzles and other toys that call for putting-together skills. The interest and stimulation that puzzles arouse will help build resourcefulness, and our grandchildren will need to be resourceful in the years to come.

Life's puzzles can begin early. Children face adjustments even in the most stable of families and in the best of day-care facilities and schools: how to get along with big people, how to please them, how to have fun, how to do well in school. As adults we are conscious of challenges when they come: working on relationships, solving financial difficulties, ordering a given day for its best use. Children are seldom consciously well-informed in the same way—they are often unaware of what we adults face daily, of the work that goes into putting life together and keeping it going—but children sense tensions readily enough.

Certainly this is true of major problems. One major puzzle for children is divorce and the web of relationships that often surround it. One child I'm aware of is about to get used to her third father. Unless there has been overt abuse that children have observed or experienced, the roots of divorce are a confusing mystery. Serious and patient efforts to give children substantial answers to "Why?" are hard to come by when adult emotions are high, energies are low, and even parents are confused.

In any family crisis grandmas are sometimes in the best place to be positive and supportive. The presence of a grandma can be calming in such situations, smoothing the ruffles of weary parents, of a hurting child, of competitive siblings, helping things fit together again.

A few skills make puzzle-solving easier whether it's a toy or real life: curiosity, collaboration, persistence with patience, and dealing with a missing piece. Curiosity is an indispensable ingredient in putting things together, in making sense of whatever is a challenge. My son, who teaches earth science and chemistry in high school, lamented the lack of curiosity in many students. A cousin in elementary education in another state wrote that her students were incurious. Interest in asking questions is indispensable in solving puzzles: "Where does this piece fit?" "What color matches this?" "How do I approach this thing?" Learning calls for curiosity, and when curiosity over a puzzle or a problem dies it's because the puzzle has been solved too many times and is boring, or the solution remains beyond reach, or television has consumed it—a TV-addicted child does not need curiosity.

Grandmas can stimulate curiosity: a small stroll in the neighborhood to look at what's growing (even a weed coming up in a sidewalk is of interest), a trip to a museum, aquarium, or zoo are all ways to open doors in a child's mind.

Some parents make it clear that curiosity is dangerous, but by seeking to be protective, a price is paid in stifling the desire to learn. Adults can curb curiosity by ignoring "Why?" When asking "why" continues to an absurd point, a laugh is better than "Quit asking me why." If parents do discourage an interest in the world, a grandma can free curiosity through many avenues, including a cheerfulness about "Why?" even if she doesn't know the answer.

Another skill in puzzle-solving is collaboration. Taking it on and doing it together is efficient and encouraging. A companionable effort helps the solution come faster. A grandma is often free to be part of this team effort in play and in life, and the challenge to grandmas is to come alongside without taking over. I solved a construction problem for C. J. when he was four, and was rewarded with his disappointment: "I didn't help." There's a need to do some observing before entering an activity—even when invited, one should ease in. "I can do it myself" is a strong hands-off signal unless it turns out the child has really taken on more than he can handle. A certain level of frustration will tell us that help is needed.

When a grandma is present, her steadiness is itself a "coming alongside." Sometimes a way to lighten a load for children is to ease the load for parents: sewing something (most grandmas can do that even though the skill is disappearing), driving someone somewhere, pitching in wherever it's called for—these activities suggest themselves when we're willing to collaborate. There are times grandmas can provide a welcome distraction from an especially busy or tense household by offering what a particular child likes best to do: playing a game, reading aloud, taking a walk.

An active interest in a grandchild's current craze is not only an aspect of collaboration, but a way to keep us informed about his world. Seeking to understand the content of a favorite TV program, video game, or book that is outside the range of our own pleasure is a small concession toward cooperation in their lives. Children may sense when an activity doesn't appeal to us, but it's a gift from grandma to continue the interest, letting them do their own evaluation in light of their growing understanding of what is valuable and what is not. The whole matter of collaboration, adding our presence and ability to the mix, is at least in part a matter of who we are, the kind of persons we have come to be as we enter into these special lives.

Persistence with patience is another puzzle-solving aid. Something unfinished seems to call for completion, then or later. Satisfaction comes with "Done!" A family vacation jigsaw could be left and tackled again, growing at an uneven pace, but we tried to finish it before we left for home. When a child's interest wanes, grandma can gently push for completion or suggest finishing it later.

We persist when we pick up unfinished conversations with our grandchildren, or when we sense a problem has not been solved and can be addressed again. Patience is called for when we continue to provide a spirit of non-judgment in the face of all the activity around us, even when it isn't of our making.

A more subtle puzzle-solving skill involves a missing piece. Can we finish even if a piece is not there? Does the disappointment take away the pleasure? Can the elusive piece be imagined? At my instigation, six-year-old Andrew and I had almost completed a jigsaw map of the United States only to find West Virginia missing, lost somewhere. We talked about the states surrounding the missing piece and imagined what color it might have been. Andrew accepted that a piece was missing, but the puzzle was almost too much: "Too many states," he said. In our affluence we tend to toss out an incomplete puzzle instead of valuing every piece. A grandma can help grandchildren to accept a missing piece in the same spirit that they can learn to handle any other missing goods of life.

The colors and shapes of jigsaws always end up going together smoothly; sometimes this is true of life, sometimes not. I am by no means privy to most of the challenges that come to my grandchildren, but I become aware of some while I look on, and hints of others come one way and another. Puzzle-play, as children grow, becomes problem-solving in life.

C. J., not long ago, had been watching a cartoon before I realized he was viewing refugees leaving Kosovo, people of all ages moving along impossibly impeded. It was not a physically violent picture (certainly not to match that of most cartoons) and I didn't interrupt even though the emotional violence was there. When I remarked that it was sad he turned and nodded, his face stricken. He was confronting a major puzzle at just that age when reality comes far more clearly into focus. Children are not exempt in our day from earthly terrors.

My daughter mentioned that the teenage chatter in the car was silenced the day after the shootings at Columbine High. While close encounters with violence may not be part of the world for grandmas reading this book, stress related to violence is a national issue. There are 22 million children in the United States between the ages of twelve and seventeen of which 5.7 million have been victims of either serious sexual or physical assault, and 9 million have witnessed serious violence: that's over half of children in that age range.[1] One teacher, after a shooting death of a student, went from desk to desk listening and talking as students shared their own stories. Later she said, "I felt like we were living on different planets." We inhabit one planet, however, and the "depression, anxiety, post-traumatic stress disorder, [and] alcohol and drug abuse [that have] significantly lowered academic achievement" is a violence-related legacy we will *all* share in the future.[2] We seem quite willing to allow easy gun procurement knowing that guns kill people.

All of our grandchildren face the potential of difficult and even dangerous puzzles on any given day. Children who are confronted with cancer, cerebral palsy, and other very challenging problems may see life as a blank wall. The perfect fit between who they are and what the future holds can be enormously complicated. As a small-statured person, my grandson Andrew faces life with the pieces of an absorbing puzzle certainly not put together, but he is hedged about with wise parents and caring aunts, uncles, cousins, and grandparents and is doing very well. Grandmas can help to lower the barriers of frustration with a kind of reimagining—first, to see the child through God's eyes, and then to help the child see himself as a perfect fit in God's sight. We have the privilege of representing God, in part, to our grandchildren.

Children need to understand that one day God will make sense of the inequities, injustices, and tragedies of this world; someday God will bring life's puzzles to a satisfactory conclusion. This is not playing Pollyanna. If we know God in Jesus Christ, we know God's character; God will not forever endure the sin that we know creates enormous suffering world-wide. Grandmas can be part of such reinforcement when the opportunities come. Our presence, phone calls, notes, postcards, and small gifts express solidarity as grands grow to face and handle the pieces of the big puzzle.

One of my sons expressed his dismay that Casey and Matthew at two and one are not yet old enough to remember what they're seeing and hearing and doing on various carefully planned outings. Neither will little children remember how a grandma has played with them, but strength for the future is built into them through these efforts of parents and grandparents; each positive experience will add resources to their lives for later use with the puzzles life brings.

When puzzles present themselves, prayer is crucial.[3] In prayer we can enlarge from one child to many. A prayer for C. J.'s heart to be expanded upon seeing the suffering of others grew to a prayer for all children who are suffering now—the millions of street children of our world, or the many children forced to head households in Rwanda after the genocide and in Zambia where AIDS has taken the lives of scores of parents, or the children whose lives are stunted in sweat-shops. Prayer for my short-statured grandson expands to include all those who are faced with dwarfism and its attending physical and other life-centered problems.

Prayers for my teenage grandchildren grow into prayer for all youth from homes where positive values have been carefully demonstrated by example and guidance. These young people can make a significant contribution to our country and to the world now and in the future. We can offer prayer for all the teenagers who are angry and without direction. Since one-third of the world's population is under the age of fifteen, we'd better pray for children and teenagers everywhere. Certainly a Christian grandmother's world reaches far beyond her own family.

Grandma Her Self

You as a grandmother have your own personal puzzles—each of us knows her own world and what we need to work on. Perhaps the pieces are all there and simply need some rearranging—time is not used the way you'd like, or your personal effects need sorting, or something in your home is unfinished that would give you much satisfaction if you could say, like a completed puzzle, "Done!" Perhaps the pieces are scattered and need collecting—a relationship could use mending: a phone call made, a letter written, a gift sent. You alone are the evaluator of your puzzles, and they do come in many shapes and sizes.

No matter what form your puzzles take, the puzzle-solving skills we use with children will always help. *Curiosity* will keep you thinking creatively about a solution—not dwelling on a problem in resignation, but thinking of some new approach. Some new ideas about what to do will no doubt call for some *patience with persistence,* especially if the solution means coming to terms with your own behaviors or mending a relationship. *Collaboration* is a necessity much of the time as it connects us to those who can help us. God as Collaborator works most often by bringing others into our lives. As we age, we will become increasingly well acquainted with the need to *handle a missing piece,* such as the loss of good health.

Some of your puzzles are extensions of those that confront your grandchildren: the state of their health, how they fare in the schools they attend, what direction their energies will take, how they will handle defeats that come, who will be genuinely good friends for them, their ups and downs. The more you are involved in your grandchildren's lives, the more you will feel their puzzles as your own.

We live in a world that challenges us with countless puzzles. One gift that grandmas bring to grandchildren is helping them learn the skills to solve the various puzzles of childhood. Providing hope and prayer for those who must wait to have their puzzles solved is one of a grandmother's most fundamental spiritual vocations. Our personal puzzles are indeed significant. Curiosity, patience with persistence, and collaboration will help grandmas and grandchildren find solutions to the missing pieces and other challenges of life.

Notes

1. "Children's Legacy of Violence," *Los Angeles Times,* 28 September 1999.

2. Ibid.

3. Richard Foster, *Prayer: Finding the Heart's True Home* (San Francisco: Harper, 1992), is the best book on prayer I have read. He gently introduces us to "the huge forest of prayer and names each tree, points out what is distinctive in each bush and flower," to quote the kudo on the back cover.

Four

COLORING

(Living Inside and Outside Expectations)

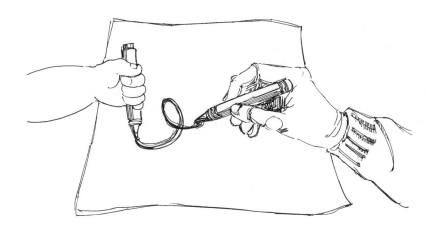

The Game

Coloring is gentle play and I have fond memories of satisfying sessions featuring color books and crayons with Ian, Leslie, C. J., and Andrew when they were five or six. Choosing shades, swapping colors, and discussing our subject matter were companionable. All inside the lines, our work had a certain discipline. They were happy cooperative efforts.

Coloring can certainly go amiss. Little-child coloring efforts were not much fun. Madison at two turned the page every time I began to color a ball red or a tree green, which is just as well as she tended to scribble over them. Deanna, when a little older, could find something more intriguing farther on in the book. This will continue to happen as Casey, Steven, and Matthew get old enough to color with me. Felt markers seep through most coloring books. Broken crayons lack pizzazz. Pictures can be too simple or too hard.

Finishing inside the lines can be very satisfying. We have overcome a tendency to be sloppy. We have a real picture and not a scribble. That is the goal in a coloring book. But even as we applaud the well-colored picture we know that coloring outside the lines is an attractive possibility. "It's more fun to color outside the lines," was among the items in a piece by Ann Landers listing "important things my kids taught me."[1] There's a time for coloring inside the lines, and a time when the lines need not be honored.

Grandmas and Grandchildren

The connection between coloring inside the lines and obedience is easy to make. There's much in print and from pulpits these days warning us that our society is too permissive, that children must indeed learn the self-discipline of "inside the lines" and the strength to obey.

Obedience sometimes takes strength, and obedience to God is paramount. What is difficult is knowing God well enough to be sure what we are required to do. Our grandchildren face the life-long challenge of knowing when coloring inside the lines is important, and when it's all right, even good, to color outside the lines, to make their own statements as they seek to discern which lines are God's and which lines are not. Grandmas can play an important role in this process.

Part of coloring inside the lines for a child is to follow parental guidelines, both stated and subliminal—children sense as well as hear what a parent wants. Children work hard from an early age to please parents; it takes little longer than a first birthday for a toddler to realize clearly what parents expect and what will make them happy. When these clear guidelines are breached and a child "colors outside the lines," grandmothers sense it more quickly, perhaps, than we did with our own as little ones.

Grandmas can give a great gift to children by warmly accepting them where they are in their "coloring." There is absolutely no need for a grandma to add her own opinions or expectations to that of the parents. There will be no lasting warmth toward a grandma who requires pleasing all of the time. A child tries to make peace with parents but probably won't use the same energy on grandmas. Without disparaging our worth, we are not one of life's daily necessities unless we are full-time caregivers.

My own grandmother managed to treat me very differently than she did her own daughter, my mother. She had been a very strong and culturally conservative officer in the Salvation Army. She had rules and parameters for her daughter and sons that were difficult for them to handle with the joy that should be part of childhood. My mother's reading was closely monitored, movies were out, activities were limited, careful conservative dress was required.

Determined as she was that things should be different for us, my mother lived with major tensions, able with her mind to move past those legally binding childhood days, but not with her emotions. My grandparents had carried out their restrictions in the name of love, but my uncles left the church and my mother's dedication to God was not without conflict.

My mother's cousin, now an elderly woman, remembers warm and happy times in the home of my grandparents. This was because an aunt and uncle were not required to levy restrictions on the child of someone else. So it is with grandmas! We can see things in new ways with our grand-children and allow them to explore new interests with us.

By the time I came along, my grandma had softened and knew she need not be my disciplinarian. I'm grateful for the contented hours sitting at her big wooden kitchen table with permission to make holes in the end of it using whatever blunt instruments were at hand, for climbing almond trees, for Bible stories told in pleasant settings. That's what a grandmother can be and do in the life of a grandchild: she can give as much freedom as possible without judgments.

There's much to be said for coloring inside the lines. Following family patterns of order makes life peaceable. It is obvious that grandmas can do lots to encourage keeping rooms neat or carrying one's own weight with household jobs. Doing well in school is admirable as long as a child is effectively stimulated—no child can learn much by refusing to cooperate. Expressing pride in school accomplishment comes very naturally for a grandma! Our Andrew is just beginning first grade and as I talked to him about the start of school he remonstrated about home-work—he'd had a taste of it in kindergarten. It wasn't hard to remind him of the good work he'd done that kinder-garten year and the fine certificates on his bedroom wall such as "Student of the Month" and "Perfect Attendance, Month of May." I confess to an uneasiness with the bumper sticker that reads, "My Child is an Honor Student at Midvale Junior High," but it doesn't, obviously, keep me from pride in my own grandchildren short of advertising it to the world!

Children can begin coloring outside the lines, opposing the will of parents, without being aware of it and tensions can rise. I know of an ardent feminist, an intelligent woman who has thought through the difficult gender issues of our day. She determined that her daughter would not be programmed into lacy pink dresses, ruffles, bows, and patent leather shoes. Imagine her chagrin when her little girl turned out to have a profound attraction for these very things! A father's heart can be set on his son excelling in baseball and become unhappy because the son sticks to curiosity about the way things work and golf is the only sport that interests him. The girl and the boy color outside the lines of parental expectations.

In these situations a grandma who is observant is free to support quietly and to encourage. This encouragement is not done in opposition to a parent, but with a deep understanding of both the parent and the child. Our own perhaps unreasonable expectations are not so far behind us that we can't remember how parents feel! Our role is neither to join in league with parents or to oppose them, but to open up a loving space where stereotypes can be stretched a bit for our grandchildren.

Grandmas can also help where the "line-drawing" of siblings is constricting a child's development. Older siblings sometimes have agendas in mind for younger brothers or sisters. A sister can be conflicted between her own ideas about her appearance and a desire to please an admired older sister or brother. "Maybe," grandma says, offhand, "Suzy likes her hair short," and a simple confirming statement has quietly given Suzy some confidence in her own judgment.

Sibling rivalry is always a possibility and can begin early. Living in a small town in North Dakota when our first three children arrived, I relied heavily on Dr. Benjamin Spock's *Baby and Child Care* in which he cautioned that jealousy when a baby arrives is inevitable and needs to be softened by lots of attention all around. My great-niece Petra, who is three, was recently joined by a new baby brother. Not many days later her mother suggested she and Petra could resume their habit of early morning walks, with Gus on her back. "Yes," said Petra happily, "and we can pretend it's just us!"

Teasing that appears harmless at first can become destructive when one sibling constantly badgers a brother or sister. Teasing about a child's person or activities can cause the child to doubt his or her basic worth. A girl, now grown, was teased unmercifully over a period of years— her life was constantly punctuated by the slings and arrows of her older brother; their mother seemed not to want to interfere. Now, as adults, these siblings have very little to do with each other. Firm words from a grandma might have made a difference.

The freedom to color inside or outside the lines can allow a child to discover all his or her potential. The fourth grade experience of a friend in her class during an art lesson offers a parable of coloring inside and outside the lines. Starting with a blank piece of art paper and using charcoal pencils, students drew squiggles for two minutes over the surface in any and all directions. They examined the squiggles from all angles to see if a potential picture appeared, at which point the emerging picture was reinforced with heavy lines and the rest dulled with charcoal eraser. The one she kept and framed was of a woman sweeping up garbage. The squiggles are like the child's freedom to color, the examination and out-lining like the emerging unique young person.

Children and teenagers must exercise trial and error in order to discern their own true identity and interests. Preparation for adulthood requires us to try on many hats. Sometimes it's hard for a young person to exercise freedom in career direction: it can seem like coloring outside the lines. Firm, repeated, and rather public statements from parents (or a grandma) bearing on a child's future can limit freedom. "Justin is the family artist—he'll do great things." "Sammy's going to be a doctor. Isn't that wonderful?"

"Carrie wants to be a missionary when she grows up—we are so proud of her!" Better responses might be: "Justin does love to draw," or "Sammy admires Dr. Smith," or "Carrie is interested in what missionaries do." If a child's early vocational direction is a genuine call from God, he or she doesn't need constant adult reinforcing. Holding a young person accountable to what was communicated at one time in some early enthusiasm may lead to confusion and constriction. In the desire to please and to conform, a young person can move in a direction that may not be God's best for him or her. Acceptance or encouragement of new interests is called for even if, for the parents or the grandparents, it is coloring outside the lines.

Sometimes there is a pain-filled side to this matter of coloring. Coloring inside the lines can be destructive when obedience is forced at the expense of a child's emerging sense of self. We are increasingly aware of the sexual abuse of children, but there are more subtle ways in which our human sexuality can be smothered by powerful people (parents, relatives, or others). The frowning communication that sex is dirty can result in a life shadowed by shame: shame can shape life in a way that it may take years to overcome. Tremendous courage is needed to learn how to color outside those lines and to overcome such programming. A grandmother who is herself free from such shame may intervene for the health of a child. In all instances, grandma herself can be a safe place and sometimes in the case of overt abuse grandma's house can be a harbor—safe from abuse and safe for re-creating what shame and abuse have taken away.

Some Christian churches are guilty of spiritual abuse with the demand for obedience to a rigid code of behavior that lacks real biblical authority. Jesus was so full of grace. He broke rigid Sabbath rules, healing and allowing his disciples to pick grain on that holy day. He overlooked strict social custom by eating with sinners, people whom the religious leaders despised—in those days righteous people only ate with other righteous people. When Jesus drove the money changers from the temple area he was way outside the lines! If we examine the Gospel accounts thoughtfully we'll probably find that Jesus doesn't always live up to our own ideas of how to color correctly.

God's commitment to those who are on the fringes of our world is a call we can't ignore, and God's love of justice can help us understand that coloring outside the lines can be wonderfully positive. A friend, who was born in the Netherlands at the outset of the five-year Nazi occupation, writes of meeting a Jewish taxi driver, who was also Dutch, in New York years later. He told her about his deliverance as a child, which took place because a whole village colored outside the lines.

> [P]eople hid me in the village of Z. There were a lot of us there. Everybody knew the Jewish children, but we all survived because no one would tell. . . . There were suspicions. . . . They even took one of the leaders of the Underground. . . . They tortured him. He would not tell. They continued to torture him, and still he would not tell. They finally killed him.[2]

He went on to tell her that this leader's picture was in his home, and his children had sworn to honor it after he was gone.

Thoughtful people of conviction, breaking state laws in our country in the '60s, entered the conflict against racial segregation in the civil rights marches, resisting authority while seeking to break segregation, and some died. In later years some alert patriots saw the need to take illegal action against the war in Vietnam. Not long ago in our community some people, in recognition of the anniversary of the destruction of Hiroshima and Nagasaki, demonstrated near the Naval Weapons Station on behalf of the ratification of the Nuclear Test Ban Treaty. It didn't take much boldness, and they didn't break any laws, but the action fell outside the kind of behavior most of us expect. The well-informed grandma knows we could draw up a long list of injustices in our world. In the future of our own country our grandchildren may be called to color outside the lines, to perform, perhaps, some act of civil disobedience in the cause of justice. Grandmas can nurture the space for this kind of living.

Grandma Her Self

Do you sometimes find you are coloring both inside and outside the lines? Maybe you speak up about your political views when you are with friends—if they agree with you, you are coloring inside the lines; should they disagree they will think you are coloring a little wildly. Perhaps our grown children have an agenda for our days and would rather we didn't stray off the picture that we're coloring. We have choices, regardless of friends or family.

It can be uncomfortable to make noise about injustice, but there are things grandmothers can do to help effect changes that aim at God's commitment. Letters to senators or representatives or state legislators are effective and can be simple statements in our own words of what we would like to see happen. Even though my grandchildren may not see me writing such letters, my convictions are communicated to them when these subjects come up. School-age children are interested these days in the environment, and they usually reflect the parents' views in presidential elections—grandmas can build on these interests.

The musician Ken Medema, with his well-tuned concern for social justice, wrote a song that stirs my grandmotherly heart and leaves me thinking of more youthful days. Much of the power of the song is lost on paper, but here is the chorus:

> Walk down the narrow highway,
> Run down the road less traveled,
> Step on the foaming wave and leave that boat behind.
> Go where the brave dare not go
> Learn what the wise dare not know
> Follow the cross before you color outside the lines.[3]

You can make a difference in the lives of your grandchildren as you live out your own convictions, accept the children where they are, encourage them in appropriate freedoms, help them to sustain the sense of justice they're born with. (What child does not know what fairness is?) Grandchildren will observe how we respond with courtesy to store clerks and other service people, they will sense whether we are committed to racial equality, they will grow up knowing if we are informed about and resistant to injustice. We may simply reinforce these qualities in their parents, but it is possible that we will present a different witness to them.

Grandchildren will know whether our faith is set in cement or if we are free to hear the Holy Spirit speak to us in bold new ways. Later on, when issues arise, they will be free to make their own thoughtful judgments, to understand the bigger picture, and to follow the cross wherever it leads them, coloring after God's own heart. Grandma will have been a force for God's greater good.

Notes

1. *Los Angeles Times*, 15 October 1999, Ann Landers column.

2. Johanna W. H. van Wijk-Bos, *Reformed and Feminist* (Louisville: Westminster/John Knox Press, 1991), 15.

3. Ken Medema, "Color Outside the Lines." Copyright 1996 Brier Patch Music, 4324 Canal, Grandville, Michigan.

Five

SORRY

(Managing the Musts)

The Game

SORRY has been around my house for a long time, and by a happy chance in our somewhat careless game-keeping, all the markers and cards are intact. If you win at SORRY it's mostly in spite of yourself. SORRY allows a minimum of choice. You must take a card, and all the cards you take say "You must . . ."

"—move one man backward 4 squares."
"—move one man forward 8 squares."

The SORRY card itself reads: "Must take one man from your start, place it on any square that is occupied by any opponent, and return that opponent's man to its start."

The only decision is which of your opponent's men to send back. We are happy to draw a SORRY card—we laugh and say, "So sorry!"

SORRY isn't a game for little children. My niece in her pre-teens and I had a championship tournament. I played it yesterday with C. J., who is eight, and we were close but I won, crowed a bit, and he laughed. I know he's a good sport and asked him about it.

"It doesn't matter," he said.

"You mean you don't care if you win?"

"Well, I know you can't always win a board game. No one's perfect . . . except God."

Grandmas and Grandchildren

The point of this chapter is not to apologize, saying "I'm sorry," but to encourage grandchildren to do what they must in life. Like the game SORRY, the grandma who is committed to being available to her grandchildren will draw many Must cards. "Needs must" is a favorite phrase of an elderly cousin, and there are plenty of times when a grandma needs to do a Must. It's our turn, and the card we are in the act of pulling reads: "Must move directly with available energy and other resources."

Musts include minor everyday acts like giving a glass of water when a child is thirsty, or adding a Band-Aid to real or imaginary ills. Must can mean making a major move: a friend flew suddenly to Africa when a grandchild was born and her daughter's life hung in the balance. There are many more or less dramatic situations in which a grandmother can assume a helping role.

We grandmas can support the Musts of grandchildren.

The ordinary Musts for grandchildren under school age are the everyday activities that are essential so they can grow in well-being: they must dress, eat, sleep, and use awake time in pleasant and constructive ways.

Sometimes grandmothers have to relearn the Musts of child care. My mother wrote me on the birth of our first child, "Eternal vigilance!" but that was a long time ago, so grandma's reeducation proceeds apace. Some Musts one doesn't forget; some call for a reminder.

- A hand must always be held while crossing the street—not yours by the child, but the child's by yours.
- Sunblock must go on before an outing to the beach or playground.
- Small objects capable of choking a crawler must be kept out of reach.
- Cooking must be done on back burners.
- Knives must be placed out of reach on kitchen counters.

Grandma's home may need renewed attention.

- Protectors must go into electric outlets.
- Pillows must go down on brick corners around the fireplace.
- A gate must go up at the bottom of the stairs (or else furniture might move there mysteriously).

Another kind of Must has more to do with our attitudes than safety precautions.

- Check with Moms or Dads before giving sweet treats.
- Check about gift-giving, perhaps especially the gift of cash.
- Don't violate family confidentialities.
- Don't give advice unless it's asked for (and you may have discovered already that it isn't asked for often, that is, hardly ever).

- Stay out of family controversies. Let your conversation be with God. If you can't keep quiet, leave the room.
- Try not to take sides. It's difficult not to have an opinion at least in your head, but develop the art of seeing it both ways. This is easier for some personalities; I happen to see things in shades of gray so it is not too hard for me.
- Watch for your defenses on the rise and talk them down inside yourself; defending oneself is often second-nature.

Must has these and other attitude flavors. You wind up anxious and bothered if you do not make attitude adjustments. For instance, I must take care of Madison today—that is, I voluntarily made myself available and her mother really must work this shift at the hospital. I can determine a series of cheerfully executed things to do with her, or hope against the odds she'll be happy enough with her toys to let me get on with a most intriguing book or a demanding project of my own. I may not be able to make my own move in this life-game for several hours, and I need to resolve that this is okay.

The Musts that children sometimes draw for us can be two-edged surprises. One early afternoon my daughter took Deanna from day care to spend a few hours with her and Grandma, before adding a little brother to the mix. We had envisioned a happy three-way girl time. It was soon apparent that Grandma wasn't welcome on this small outing. "But I don't want Grandma to go, I want Mommy time" was how Deanna put it. Mentally blessing Dr. Spock for warning me never to let a child hurt my feelings, I quickly acquiesced and they dropped me off at the house, feeling only slightly overlooked and quickly molified by a good book. The games Deanna and I cheerfully played that evening meant that all was well between us.

Later as I mentally processed the afternoon's events, I felt like a winner. We may discover that we do not always have the unconditional positive regard of our grands. In this playing out of life, emotional time with mother when you have been in day care is essential and time with grandma is not. Grandmothers have an important role in a family setting, but we are not the primary emotional partners for our grandchildren.

The necessity for day care outside the home calls for a demanding set of Musts. Children must be out of the house and on the way to day care at the hour parents must leave for work. I know grandmas who take on the day-care role, and they alone can evaluate and work out what this costs in time and energy. Others of us are sometimes in a position to help.

The half hour after parents and children arrive home from work and day care is perhaps the most challenging: The transition from work to home offers parents a brief respite from one set of responsibilities only to plunge into another. Everyone is tired and hungry. Working-away-from-home parents who put personal needs aside to give themselves to the well-being of their children at home are heroes. If a grandma chooses to be involved in this partic-ular Must, assistance can take the form of whatever eases tensions for parents and children: preparing a meal, fixing lunches for the following day, laundry, pet care, straight-ening, grocery shopping, or whatever a family's need and one's imagination brings to mind. This kind of support can allow parents some quality time with the children they haven't seen all day.

Some life situations call an older child to take on a sobering task, to do what has to be done: the care of a sib-ling, more time at household chores than at play, perhaps earning some money in order to help the family. When these Musts arise, grandmas can give encouragement and praise. For one reason or another (divorce, economic circumstances, family illness) children are sometimes thrust into roles they didn't choose. In the movie *Tea with Mussolini*, the boy Luca, who has been cared for by four older English women living in Italy, is sent to Austria to learn German by his cold and opportunistic father at the onset of World War II. The women come to the train station to see him off, and as the train pulls out there they are, scarves and handkerchiefs flying, full of smiles and chorusing pieces of advice and encouragement. Luca smiles, too, and returns their good wishes and farewells. It's a lovely picture of how caring grandmothers and grandmother-types can help a child with painful Musts.

I have found there are Musts for a grandmother when visiting that make for success even though they may intrude on the ways we usually spend our days.

- Let the day unfold without insisting on your agenda.
- Fall in with plans, unless they are beyond your physical capacity.
- Help when it seems needed; if unsure, ask if what you think is helpful really is.
- Be graciously available, without taking charge, in some area of your expertise: cooking, story-reading, the laundry, cleaning, shopping, or some other skill you possess.
- Pray, on the spot and/or in your own quiet space. Most hosts try to make some quiet time for grandmothers, so some of us will have it. Others will not have this luxury.

Flexibility in carrying out the Musts, whether we are visiting or entertaining our families at home, is a quality that pays off both physically and emotionally. Flexibility helps create an atmosphere of ease and peace. If the agenda is punctuated by our inflexibility, which translates to tensions and hurt feelings, we have not done well. We are not children and we are no longer primarily parents, we've graduated to the next generation and we are super-adults. We are the parent of a parent but we have abandoned the parental role so that our children can make use of all that they've received from us in years past.

It is my experience that prayer becomes crucial with our Musts. When the Musts go beyond those required in ordinary times and seem to take more energy than we think we have, we can be conscious of God's role as Energizer. In his book on prayer, Richard Foster suggests that we can see our actions in response to the Musts as prayers in and of themselves.

> Each activity of daily life in which we stretch ourselves
> on behalf of others is a prayer of action.[1]

For grandmothers these action-prayers might involve cutting off sleep at one end of the day or moving to meet a need when our own legs are ready to sit. It might mean reading a book a child has chosen that we've already read to sheer boredom, or seeking inner quiet when the noise is pretty loud. To think that such acts as these are actual prayers is a big boost!

One of the most challenging things to do is coming to the support of families, and especially grandchildren, when divorce happens. One out of two marriages in our country ends in divorce so many grandparents face the pain and demands divorce detonates. Grandfathers can and do enter into this too-frequent and terrible situation, but it's grandmothers who often take the initiative, take the most active role, and keep the help in motion.

In her book *Helping Your Grandchildren through Their Parents' Divorce*, Joan Schrager Cohen quotes a grandparent as saying, "When their parents divorce, the children lose their center." Cohen says this about grandparents:

Grandparents are accustomed to the variables and injustices of life. They have learned to cope with adversity and know all about the fragility of life. Building on cumulative life experiences, they can, as the true "grown-ups" in this unfolding drama, become teachers or role models to their grandchildren (and children). During the various stages of divorce, grandchildren are desperately seeking mentors. Grandparents can help build their grandchildren's confidence and competency. More important, they can offer them a positive outlook on life.[2]

Cohen wrote this book when she and her husband were confronted with their daughter's divorce; the book contains insight into the pain of divorce itself, and provides very practical ways grandparents can help a family toward healing. Their own sacrifice (my term, not hers) stretched over geographical distance and involved emotional and physical challenges.

Unfortunately, there are grandparents who remove themselves from their families during divorce or adopt the face of indifference, unable for whatever reason to face or address the pain. Instead we can hold our beloved children and grandchildren through the pain of this crisis while letting our lives and life-span serve as gentle reminders that renewal is possible. There can be fullness of life beyond divorce through hope, prayer, and courageous living.

Another Must that some grandparents are dealt is the geographical separation that occurs when they live countries away, if not continents, serving the church or working in a foreign-related business. They are getting older and one day will be back "home," but the child-years of their grandchildren will be over. Sometimes grown children and their families are away in foreign countries while we are here. My own freedom to be with any of my families within a few hours is a great privilege in light of those who are unable to take a hands-on grandmother role. Since time and distance from God's perspective are as nothing, wherever we or our loved ones are, God is there—that truth may provide some comfort against the human reality of distance.

Mail service seems to be increasingly efficient in most faraway places; long-distant e-mail is impressive. Efforts to communicate pay large dividends in grandchildren's lives, and a little goes a long way. It's easy to send a post card, airmailed, that says only, "I love you." Habit plays its part: a sort of background consciousness about communicating becomes habitual. Carelessness can set in with distance. Distance can become an excuse for not communicating; perhaps the pain of separation is eased by "forgetting" to work at it. Distance that can't be easily bridged is eased by frequent prayer for children and grandchildren.

Grandma Her Self

A must for a Christian grandmother is a clear call to respond if response is possible; Christ calls you to serve at times when it isn't easy. Problems can arise if you yourself are going through a personally challenging time. It can be hard to accommodate oneself gracefully to the Musts of family, meeting them where *they* are in demanding times, when self is shouting for attention. Your own needs may preclude stepping in to help. It's important to be honest about what you can and can't do, and to be ready to say "No" when the energy or time is just not there. It's a deeply personal thing, this kind of decision-making, and when you have generally been available there is the hope that a refusal will be respected, not only in the moment, but with grace.

Jesus said, after his invitation "Come to me," that his yoke is easy and his burden is light. If you feel excessively weighed down or used by your families because you haven't been wise about refusals, anger comes sneaking up and there's trouble ahead. It's time to rethink your attitude to life's Musts. The easy yoke and the light burden mean that God's grace is very present and bigger than the burdens that Musts tend to hand us; sometimes a "No" can bring a sense of freedom and allow the spirit of grace to flow. When you say "Yes," your services become those prayers of action; when you say "No" you preserve the spirit of grace in which we do stand. "No" can bring a sense of freedom that doesn't change your relationship to our gracious God and it helps your family to see you clearly as your own person.

The game SORRY is fun to play; in life the Musts can be demanding, but they can bring their share of satisfaction. We have done what we can when the need arises. We are there on behalf of our grandchildren whether we are with them or away from them, and they will know that because they have known our presence in demanding times.

Notes

1. Richard J. Foster, *Prayer: Finding the Heart's True Home,* 174.

2. Joan Schrager Cohen, *Helping Your Grandchildren through Their Parents' Divorce* (New York: Walker and Company, 1994), 3.

Six

IMAGINATION

(Coming Alive Inside)

The Game

Imagination is make-believe. Imagination goes beyond our five senses and it brings life into being where there was no life. When we imagine, we have something that wasn't there before. Imagination can stir our hearts and light up our lives. Imagination can even lengthen our days because our bodies respond positively to the fun and joy it brings.

God's imagination lies beyond telling. God created time, and in the time it took to complete the universe we have what overwhelms the most creative human thought: the abundant forms of flora and fauna and their exquisite variations on our own planet. One can imagine that God delighted in bringing life to us, each human unique, with Earth one tiny orb out of all the galaxies.

Grandmas and Grandchildren

Imagination can begin in a simple way. Just before she turned two, Casey, with a big smile, told me she was going to the store. Asked what she was going to buy, she said, "Milk and bread." I pretended to fish out money, she left the room and was soon back carrying her purchases. Did she have any money left over? Yes, and she gave me a handful of air. We played "store" for another half hour buying and selling.

Madison's favorite make-believe person-to-be is Melissa. "Grandma, pretend I'm Melissa and I'm coming to see you."

"Who shall I be?"

"You be the sister."

Two of my grandchildren played a kind of hide-and-seek calling for a very limited imagination. I sat with their legs on my lap, their heads covered, and wondered out loud, "Where is . . . ?" and then discovered a toe, no, ten toes, and an ankle, no, two, and so on, and finally learned to whom all these appendages belonged.

The small games I play with my grandchildren are only the bare bones of imagination. My sister has an on-going saga, complete with a set of made-up characters, with which she entertains her grandchildren. C. S. Lewis tells us that from early childhood his life was inhabited by make-believe: talking animals and magical kingdoms.[1] The Narnia chronicles, now fifty years old, still come to us out of his fertile imagination and are rich with insight into Christian living.

One story book illustrates how a grandma can enter into a make-believe world. A little girl, Kay, finds a magic golden leaf during leaf-raking time. This lovely leaf makes wishes come true: sand pies turn into real ones, a wish becomes a rose so big she can climb in it, bubbles reveal castles and jewels, dress-up clothes come replete with jewels and crowns, music becomes mermaids and pipers. After each of these wonderful bits of magic she goes to one or another family member to tell them, but they always say, kindly, "Yes, dear. Now run along, I'm gardening" (or raking leaves, or washing socks, and so on). Finally she goes to her grandmother who immediately says, "I see you've caught a magic leaf!"

"How did you know?" the child asks.

"Because I caught one once. It did wonderful things, but everyone was too busy to listen when I told them."

"Just like me," said Kay.

"Yes, dear," said Granny. "Just like you."[2]

Granny's imagination meets her granddaughter and identifies with her. Grandmas can always follow a child in make-believe even when one's initiative with imagination is thin. I respond to the creative overtures of my grandchildren even though I do not often begin make-believe play.

Imagination can blossom where it seems impossible; like a flower appearing through a crack in the sidewalk, we realize its beauty and power. The movie *Life is Beautiful* is a poignant use of imagination in the tragedy and horror of a concentration camp during World War II. In a sacrificial and loving way the father instills into his little son's heart that they are all playing a great game and that if they obey all the rules about hiding, terrible as they are, they will have the most points to win, and the prize will be a real tank. When the tanks of liberation roll in the boy knows they've won the game. His father is gone, but the boy has lived, and is reunited with his mother.

Books are one childhood avenue for the cultivation of imagination, and to read to a child is certainly one of the easiest and most positive contributions a grandma can make. Authors of children's story books rely to some degree on imagination. Pictures in books for little children help them make-believe, and when the time comes for books with few if any pictures, older children are able to make the words come alive in their minds. Even with pictures there's room for the addition of imagination. Madison interrupted me the other day with all kinds of comments based on what the pictures did not show.

When Leslie was two her mother said to me, "Mom, she's reading." Leslie would sit with a stack of books and go through them one by one. Of course a book is a toy—it closes and opens, it moves and it moves in two directions, every move shows something different, and none of this happens except by the whim of the child. All of the adults in my family read well, but not all of them are book-lovers, and I think this is going to be true of the grandchildren as well. Some leap at the invitation to read, some would rather play a game.

Certain scenes will always come alive: one-year-old Steven quick to get a book whenever invited; Matthew at the same age, when told to find *Go, Dogs, Go*, trots back making g-g-g-g sounds; Casey wide-eyed over books and willing to read at any time. Reading to children is a bedtime ritual in each of my families. Reading aloud within the family will always be enriching, age and reading ability not in question.

Some Christian families deny their children fairy tales because they consider them untruthful, perhaps to ensure that their children see our faith as based on facts; they fear that make-believe might undermine faith. Jesus, out of his imagination, told many stories that didn't happen: the good Samaritan, the rich man and Lazarus, the wise and crafty steward, the prodigal son, and the pearl of great price, to name only a few.

Dancing is another wonderful way imagination can enrich our lives. Always expressive, some dancing seems to be all rhythm and energy, some takes thought and inspiration. Dancing seems to be ready to blossom in people everywhere who are child-like enough. The Beach Boys' "Surfin' Safari" bubbled up one day while I was on a visit and I was treated to Casey and her dad dancing like I imagine David danced before the ark as it entered Jerusalem; David's dance was lively and joyous, not sedate and patterned. If one can get past any irreverence, the comparison isn't a bad one. The ark coming back to Jerusalem was a great occasion for celebration, daughters are worth celebrating, and God would be very pleased if lots of dads these days danced with their daughters many years before the father/daughter dance at her wedding.

I have vivid memories of Deanna and Steven dancing with their mom (and sometimes their dad) in the living room to lively or gentler music—interpretive in the most original sense with scarves and other floaty things. Before he was two Steven's repeated maneuver was a kind of march to any rhythm, elbows bent and flapping like a rooster at dawn in the company of his more graceful partners. Madison and her daddy have developed a routine that includes special steps and twirls.

I was reminded about dancing at weddings, that once the music begins, and if children are among the guests, they are out on the floor ahead of the bride and groom. At a Christmas party of Little People of America a year ago, Andrew's cousin Matthew, before he was two, was on the floor the minute dancing started—and the rest of the family followed suit. I've danced in living rooms with a newborn in my arms, slowly and sedately, of course.

Children enjoy dressing up with dancing in mind. When

Madison was two, she coined the term "Ceebrella"—"Cee" from Cinderella and her billowing ball gown, and "brella" from the magical way an umbrella unfolds: a ceebrella is any dress with swirling potential. One of my indelible memories is Leslie and a friend slowly descending the stairs in the elaborate ball gowns found by her mother at a thrift store, complete with boas and clickie shoes.

Some senior church friends go to Disneyland just to dance with the bands on certain nights. The lead in a newspaper article read "Grandmother Hoofers Hit Their Marks Anew" and told in some detail about twenty-four dancers, ages fifty-three to eighty-seven, who dance in "'The Fabulous Palm Springs Follies' which holds the Guinness world record for the oldest professional chorus line."[3] Well, there's life in us yet even if over 99 percent of us are not follies material. As someone whose legs don't work altogether properly, my hat is off to these exotic women. Imagine!

Jacques d'Amboise, "perhaps the greatest American-born dancer of his generation," retired from the New York City Ballet and started the National Dance Institute to bring dancing to school children. The end of 1999 found him finishing a seven-month hike on the Appalachian Trail, 2,160 miles from Maine to Georgia, along the way teaching his "Trail Dance" to "thousands of students, teachers, police, prisoners, professors, and just plain folks."[4] To stifle the imagination is to stop dancing, even if the dancing is only going on inside our heads.

Alert to the many ways imagination can be expressed, we grandmas do well to keep its importance in mind.

Grandma Her Self

Imagination comes to you with enlivening power. Life is robbed of its potential fullness when one's imagination lies unused. I discovered that my own creativity grew as I became involved with my grandchildren and their marvelous ways of making up what they could never experience with their five senses.

Imagination can shed light on the way you experience the people around you—you can begin to see beyond what you usually see, finding something new and different about them. If there are people who have bothered you or become boring, can you see them with God's eyes? Imagine them growing up in their situations, in the experiences they've had of which you're aware, in the circumstances in which they are now living. Perhaps the "Why?" of them will intrigue rather than annoy and you can relate to them in more patient and renewing ways.

Imagination can renew your life with God. One way to accomplish this is to pray in a way that breaks through life as it is and sees it the way God sees it. Remember Jesus' instruction about how to pray: "Thy will be done on earth as it is in heaven. . ." Imagine, in prayer, a sick friend up and about, a stressful household in peace, a lonely child with friends. Picture in your mind this kind of God-filled answer, pray for that and trust God to bring it to pass.

Another way to refresh yourself in God through imagination is to take a new look at the people in the Bible who are recorded in all their humanity, and learn how they related to God. The emotions of Bible people aren't often spelled out and we give life to them when we add what they felt. Feel Sarah's fear and sense of betrayal as Abraham put her on loan first to a Pharoah and then a king in order to save himself; feel Rebekkah's anticipation tinged with anxiety as she left home for the adventure of meeting a lover and husband; feel Leah's humiliation as she endured being the second-best wife; feel Miriam's mixture of dread and hope as she followed her baby brother in a basket on the river and later her exultation as a prophet singing of victory on the far side of the Red Sea; feel Mary's overwhelming mix of emotions as she learned she would conceive a holy child before she was Joseph's wife—shock, awe, apprehension, joy—and a few years later horror and abandonment as she stood at the cross and watched her son die; feel the excitement and dedication of the women who cast convention aside to travel with Jesus, supporting him with their funds; feel the satisfaction of Martha's sister Mary as Jesus taught her when a woman was never taught by a rabbi; feel the deep love for God of the widow who put her whole stipend into the temple treasury; feel the competency and pleasure of Lydia as she hosted the first Christians in Philippi. Perhaps Lydia was a grandma!

Our imaginations need guarding just as any gift needs to be wisely used—we can imagine illness or make trouble more vivid than necessary. We grandmas will be rewarded using imagination in positive, daily ways: imagining the sun when it's raining, the spring in winter, a sense of peace in turmoil, a light foot when stepping is a bit painful, a vision of dancing when there doesn't seem to be anything to celebrate. Coming alive inside happens when we do make-believe.

Notes

1. C. S. Lewis, *Surprised by Joy* (New York: Harcourt, Brace & Co., 1955), 6, 15.

2. Diana Wynne Jones, *Yes, Dear!* (New York: Greenwillow Books, 1992).

3. "Grandmother Hoofers Hit Their Marks Anew," *Los Angeles Times*, 1 November 1999, sec. E4.

4. Michael Ryan, "When the Dancer Came to Town," *Parade: The Sunday Newspaper Magazine*, December 19, 1999, 10.

Seven

CHUTES AND LADDERS

(Handling the Ups and Downs)

The Game

Chutes and Ladders has been with us long enough that the parents of my grandchildren enjoyed it when they were young. The board consists of squares from one to one hundred, ten to a line back and forth to the top. Pictures of slides and ladders go down and up, here and there, intersecting the squares—nine chutes and eight ladders. If you land at the beginning of a chute or a ladder, down or up you go. Whoever gets to one hundred first wins, probably having slid down slides and gone up ladders en route. Chutes and ladders are both speedy—the slides swoop and the ladders do not need to be climbed—like rockets the ascent is swift. The game could be called "Slides and Rockets."

The chutes are longer than the ladders. For example, the littlest ladder goes up from square 36 to 44, skipping eight squares, and the shortest chute runs down from 93 to 73, skipping twenty. The longest ladder goes up from 28 to 84 (that's fifty-seven) and the longest chute sends one down from 87 to 24 (that's sixty-three). Across the top of the board there are three chutes within the last ten squares; those chutes don't descend very far, but they do go down and it's scary when one has gotten that far.

Deanna had received Chutes and Ladders for her fifth birthday. I asked her father how she liked the game and he said, "Deanna doesn't like the chutes." Well, why would she? She moves along according to the spinner (numbered 1 to 6) sometimes quite slowly if she's landed often on 1 or 2, and suddenly down a chute she goes . . . tough, when one counts on winning. And with the chutes longer than the ladders, is that fair? When I played with Deanna we were both a little tired and cranky—she landed on 28, shot near the top, and missed the rest of the chutes. The game took a fortunate ten minutes. It is, however, a fun game when one is a little older.

Grandmas and Grandchildren

The chutes and ladders of life come upon us very quickly, just as in the game. The ladders are joys that bring a burst of well-being: the announcement of an engagement or wedding with which you are particularly pleased, the uneventful birth of that very special child, any surge of satisfaction with life. Serendipities lift us, those unexpected things that delight: the discovery of a mutual friend, a sudden encouragement, a special gift, a book that grips, and so on. The chutes are those sudden plunges into discouragement, sorrow, or even despair: an accident, a diagnosis, a family quarrel, a major disappointment. As happens in the game, the chutes in life can certainly seem to be more frequent and longer than the ladders.

Most chutes are caused by events òutside ourselves. We in California are aware of some of these in nature with our four seasons: earthquake, flood, fire, and drought. No thinking person can exaggerate the devastation caused by chutes over which people have no control: major earthquakes, plane crashes, hurricanes, a big dip in the stock market, and so on. Trouble can come to us outside ourselves and be disheartening or devastating.

At the moment I'm sitting in a living room looking out at a picture of serenity. The Columbia River is flowing almost imperceptibly, deep and wide. This is the last stretch of the free-flowing Columbia: the dams above don't stop the water; the dams down below do. At the moment there's not a sound. The sky is clear but for a few wisps of cloud. Canada geese fly in formation and their honking clears the silence. I am at the top of a small ladder. But clouds are coming and rain is on the way. A major limb hangs where it snapped off a tree not long ago—one would have heard it, suddenly. A few miles away scientists and engineers and managers address the presence and problem of toxic waste tanks. The very twenty-four hours of a given day anywhere have both chutes and ladders potential.

Emotional highs and lows, part of ladders and chutes, often characterize a child's day and can be short or long. The ups and downs happen every day and will happen when we are with them. Disappointments or frustrations often seem bigger to children than they do to us, and need to be listened to as though they are as big as the children seem to believe. It will not do to minimize their chutes.

A grandma can be in a special place to comfort when the child experiences a chute because it need not be part of our relationship to "fix" things. As adults we tend to shy away from "fixit" people, other adults in our lives who want to help us find "answers," and children are no different.

One day as I gently persisted toward nap-time in the face of objections, Madison said, "You are the worst grandma ever." That was a first, and so unlike her I couldn't help laughing, but the incident serves to underscore the necessity of hearing negatives with acceptance (and generally without laughter). As C. S. Lewis said, "What I like about experience is that it's such an honest thing."[1] Negatives are an honest reflection of experience and necessary if a child is to look at life squarely, and negatives will always be associated with chutes. Something unwanted has happened and it feels bad.

Though many of our grandchildren's chutes are short-lived, some chutes can take a child down to the bottom. There is no doubt about the devastation to children of divorce. The death of a parent is of course another crisis, but with death there can be a finality, a closure that divorce often evades. A friend who lived nearby was dying, and his son said to the wife, his mother, "It could be worse." Wearily she responded, "What could be worse than this?" and he replied, "You could be getting a divorce." Presence and prayer in an on-going way may be the help we can give. If distance intervenes and can't for some reason be physically bridged, phone calls, brief notes, and small gifts can help.

Ladders that bring excitement and pleasure can be short-lived; a new toy often loses its glamour quickly. How caregivers help children handle the short chutes and ladders will say something about how children will handle themselves later when the downs and ups are longer. In ups or downs a kind of calm identification on the part of grandma can keep the see-sawing from being more important than it should be. A consistent grandma, who hears negatives and positives equally well, can add serenity to a few hours.

Grandma Her Self

Most of us experience on-going things in our lives that are less than the best—head and heart come together as we work with whatever is happening. When a blow falls on you, you deal with a new truth in your life and your heart hurts. Whether it is something bad happening to a loved one, a fresh betrayal, a misunderstanding on the part of someone you care about, or your reaction to something out in the world, you feel the pain.

A Christian may soon recall that "all things work together for good for those who love God" (Romans 8:28)—this truth is a fine place to start, but it usually starts first in your head. Head and heart work together when people are mature, but for most of us it's a process from *knowing something* (in your head) to *being someone* (in your heart). A genuine integration of head and heart will allow peace to come when you are hit by an unexpected blow. It's crucial for grandmas to allow themselves to experience a chute for what it is: a chute.

Nothing keeps your heart from pounding or dismay from ricocheting inside your head when trouble comes; you are not immune to the trauma of initial shock. Remember that God suffers with us in our setbacks and sorrows. When you go down a chute, see things from God's point of view—call reality real and deal with it honestly. Give it to God, do what seems best, wait for your head and your heart to come together.

I felt the California desert earthquake in October 1999,

which registered 7.0 at the epicenter, and though I was too far away to sustain damage, I certainly knew fear and was very aware of being by myself. Of course it occurred to me that "[God's] perfect love casts out fear," but I am still learning that (1 John 4:18). Meanwhile, for a few hours, down that short chute, I wondered how I was going to live peaceably on our own major fault—with a big earthquake here liquefaction would occur (that is, the house would sink). I felt that keenly, and prayed (one certainly prays when threatened) and in a matter of a day or two the fear was gone. I may or may not feel that fear again, but if I do I'll handle it the same way.

I know a Christian, a servant of God, who is imprisoned unjustly, in this country, as the result of a false testimony. The chute delivered him way below the playing field. He is no longer young and his ministry was taken from him. But after he wrestled honestly with his anger, fear, and grief, God has turned bitterness into peace and set before him a way to serve in prison, tutoring inmates, helping them with their correspondence, with time for prayer and study, time to think about the problem of evil.

When you give negative feelings a chance to be heard, they soften and change. Emotions are not set in cement when we let them have their say: sadness, disappointment, dismay, and outright anger will be there when something bad happens. Accepted and acknowledged, these feelings can finally resolve into a quietness of mind.

If you don't feel negatives it could be because you're in the habit of denial—a habit that shortcuts our personalities. Feelings denied are stuffed down and sooner or later depression or illness will come—in some way the energy that it takes to keep negative feelings buried will rob us of physical or emotional health. Anger or fear or grief are unpleasant, but they are only destructive when they build and build. God is in the business of truth and your relationship with God will suffer if you don't feel the whole gamut of appropriate emotions when something happens to trigger them.

Paul and Silas praying and singing hymns at midnight in that primitive prison in Philippi is one example of how to behave honestly and well under great duress. They were thrown in jail in the afternoon or early evening, but the songs didn't start until midnight. They hadn't stopped believing in God, so why weren't they singing as they were put in chains? Because they felt unbearably rotten—harassed, unjustly judged, badly beaten, in great pain. It took several hours to work through all that, to allow outrage to be felt. Finally, finally, the light began to glimmer in that black place. Talking to God began, bits and pieces of a familiar hymn began to surface, one of them tried a note or two, the other responded and before long praying and singing were the new reality, real enough that all the prisoners heard. Somehow it would come out all right (Acts 16:19-25).

Allowing God to work from horror to peace isn't restricted to the Bible. In his book *God's Long Summer*, Charles Marsh tells us about the summer of 1963, in Winona, Mississippi. Mrs. Fannie Lou Hamer and three of her friends were badly beaten with fists, boots, and blackjacks in a jail and put into cells. They had been involved in trying to help black citizens get the right to vote. Marsh writes:

In her dark cell, Mrs. Hamer was left alone to bear the physical and spiritual effects of torture. . . . The next morning something happened that slowly transformed the killing despair of the jail and dispersed the power of death. . . . Song broke free. Mrs. Hamer sang:

"Paul and Silas was bound in jail, let my people go.
Had no money for to go their bail, let my people go."

Her friends too began to sing. "Church broke out . . ."[2] Mrs. Hamer knew her Bible, she knew Paul and Silas.

Grandmas are not strangers to pain we've experienced over the years, but our concerns when our own children were little are multiplied now that they have families. I think I feel just as keenly when illness or trouble visits my grandchildren. Is this common among us? I think so. Whether the chute down which we've sped into our unexpected pain is about our own life or that of a family member, we have to handle this new thing.

When we read "Let endurance have its full effect, so that you may be mature and complete, lacking in nothing," it presupposes some unhappy occurrence in our lives that calls us to hang on (James 1:4). Why else do we need endurance? We exercise endurance in the face of something going wrong. We are not usually caught up in the physical efforts of the present moment like the parents of our grandchildren and we are often less physically able to release energy in action. We have more time to think and pray, to practice the patience that endurance calls for.

The ladders, the rockets in our scenario, are easy to take. We are glad for things that bring pleasure. I was rocketed up recently by the most enthusiastic reception at the airport on the part of Deanna and Steven—the effect lasted quite some time! Those happy events shoot us up to the top of the game minimizing the start-and-stop chutes that may have preceded the ladder. Good experiences of any sort tend to level out the ordinary.

Chutes and ladders, slides and rockets, are part of daily life, and we meet them where we are. We recognize and respond to the chutes and ladders of our grandchildren, and seek to be there for them as they learn to handle their ups and downs. We want to meet our own with wisdom. Whether they are long or short, we know that God is in them with us.

Notes

1. C. S. Lewis, *Surprised by Joy* (New York: Harcourt, Brace & World, 1955), 177.

2. Charles Marsh, *God's Long Summer* (Princeton, N.J.: Princeton University Press, 1997), 21–22. In his notes to Chapter One, Marsh writes that "there is no experience in which the obliteration of one's total world occurs in a more immediate, visceral form than in calculated violence. Intense pain is world-destroying" (209). This pain subsumes the pain most of us experience.

Eight

SCRABBLE

(Playing With What You Have)

The Game

Occasionally a small grandchild will take Scrabble out of my game box, but of course can't play—the tiles appeal only momentarily and appear to have some energy of their own as they scatter. One needs a person who can spell and think "words" and really likes the game, and that seldom happens before the teens.

An English cousin who had been a teacher was convinced that spellers are born, not made. One of my sons was dragged into a Scrabble game that quickly turned hilarious—his first word was "yes" and his second "no." I should have bought that T-shirt "BAD SPELLERS OF THE WORLD, UNTIE!" Then there's the ethereal realm of the champions when not a single word on the board is recognizable.

Players are boosted or hampered by the draw—I need a "U" or a "blank" because of course *I* can't spell a "Q" word without a "U." My "Q" looks lonelier all the time, the board less friendly, and it's ten points off my score if I'm left with "Q" when someone else ends the game by using up all his tiles. Skilled players yearn to break the 400 mark and we took a picture when friend Nancy hit 409.

Risk plays its role—some players use a turn to trade most or even all tiles for a new set. Other players affect our game—robbing opportunities, blocking, challenging us from the Scrabble dictionary. Since I don't often win, I sometimes open the board up for the sake of the game, get virtually no points, and sense little appreciation for the sacrifice. But whether or not one can spell, and even with a sophisticated vocabulary, in Scrabble you work with the tiles you draw.

Grandmas and Grandchildren

Life is like Scrabble. Some people seem to handle life casually with a light hand. Some are experts making full use of what's been given. Some are hedged about by forces beyond their control. Some accomplish great things or even win unexpectedly. Some seem to enjoy making sacrifices. In all cases the game develops when the players make the best out of what they have before them on that little shelf of tiles that represents our reality. This vacation Ian hauled out the Scrabble board and announced that he didn't expect anyone could beat him, and I'm not sure if he won a single game. He's an able Scrabble player, but we do have to play with what we have and work with what's on the board.

The grandchildren represented by most grandmas reading this book live with an affluence unknown to billions in our world, and yet the things they own will not teach them to live life well. People and relationships are more important than what money can buy; grandmas can help to undergird this truth.

My own grandmother had very little money. I lived with her and my grandfather a few months during one of my parents' economic tough times and can remember her cheerful attitude and the freedom I seemed to enjoy inside her house and about her yard. I can clearly see her in her small rocker moving gently back and forth, Bible in her lap, eyes closed. She never coerced me into "devotions" but I knew she was praying for me and all her family. She was active in her church and was president of the local Women's Christian Temperance Union; I was leery of the pledge and managed not to sign it, but always knew alcohol could be an enemy.

She would never take money from the government (whatever form that took in those years of the Great Depression), and was frugal in the use of monies sent regularly to them by my uncles. She gave food to the men who knocked on the back door and was attentive to the needs of her neighbors for soup or a cake. She never bought us birthday presents, but would do up something of her own in used gift wrap. My sisters and I loved her because she loved us.

What legacy of her do I wear besides a long waist and short legs? I learned that people are more valuable than money, prayer is important and mostly private, convictions lead to action, and that these things are passed on by example rather than talk. What role will I have in the lives of the grandchildren so dear to me? In what way will I help them live well with the tiles they have drawn in life's game? I think it will come out of the consistency between who I am and what I do in Christ. My own values reviewed and reshaped to reflect what I trust are Christian values will play a role.

Grandmas are able to attend to the unique personhood of each grandchild, to the set of tiles they have drawn. What is most interesting to each one? Conversations with them can involve those special things that most capture their attention. We can also give gifts that celebrate those interests. Two of my under-sixes are more interested in games than books, so I'll buy them games. My under-threes receive small reminders that Grandma's around and waiting to see what interests develop.

Grandma Her Self

When you reach grandma-age in this game there are fewer options to trade your tiles for a new set, to acquire new saleable skills. You have your present measure of health, energy, finances, living situation, wide experience, and abilities. You have your mind, your inner world with your attitudes and ways of handling yourself. How will you work with what you have? What will be your approach to the rest of your days, limited as they are? What role does God play in your life? Perhaps what life has dealt you feels good—you have what you want, materially and with the people close to you. If there is something missing in your life, however, then who you have become, where you are now, is where you begin moving toward more satisfaction.

God met the needs of people we encounter in the Bible by working with what they had. Elisha asks the poverty-stricken widow who has cried to him for help, "What do you have?" She has only a little oil, but that's where the miracle starts. Facing a hungry crowd, Jesus asks, "What do you have?" and is presented with a few loaves and fish.

Jesus starts with these and spreads a feast. Jesus accepted people where he found them, who they already were with what they already had, and worked from there.

The wise way for you as a grandmother to play the game now, with whatever you have, is by first accepting yourself where you are. God accepts you just as you are and supports you as you do the same thing. Acceptance is not resignation, some kind of passive giving up. Acceptance is an active thing, something positive to do, and gives you the freedom to take a next step. The widow accepted her need and acted in going to Elisha. Jesus accepted the need of the crowd and actively sought an answer. Resignation did not play any part in these scenarios.

Resignation in older people is not attractive or helpful and it seems to take different forms. There's the resignation, "Things are just no good." Recently a gentleman out for exercise stopped by my yard as I was about to spray for whitefly. The conversation began with pests and went on to the jokers in Washington, the failure of our schools, the disappointment in colleagues who let him down, the granddaughter he's nervous about. It was difficult to participate in this. True or false, I choose to see the world through different eyes.

Resignation can come in the quiet silence of settled disappointment. Family has let you down, the energy to make friends is gone, defeat in the past is still unsettling, mistakes you made in life still live on, and hope is as gray as a grandma's hair. Or we can resign ourselves to physical limitations, forgetting that we can still grow on the inside. Out of resignation comes the sad but rather cranky question, "Where is God?"

Rather than become resigned to life as it is, entertain the hopeful idea of acceptance. All change begins with acceptance. Accepting yourself where you are can start very tentatively because it seems a remote and unworkable concept. You may be almost certain something about your life is not acceptable, but acceptance leads into a process that works toward the answers you seek.

Begin the process with attention to yourself in your situation. Listen to what you are saying to yourself from the world within you. We in our generation (especially we Christians) tend to equate listening to ourselves, caring for ourselves, with selfishness. Selfishness sees others only for what they can do for us; self-care is sensible. The truth is that if you don't put self first, paying close attention to the tiles you've drawn on your board in this life game, you won't be able to get on with the changes you know need to be made. The airline advice for caregivers to put oxygen masks on themselves first applies on the ground as well. You won't have the energy to be an attentive grandmother without paying attention to yourself, to your inner world.

This choice of acceptance is not made only once but needs repeating until the habit of self-judgment is replaced with the positive warmth acceptance brings. Acceptance needs to become a habit; it's a way of thinking that can, with practice, become a way of being.

Awareness comes with acceptance. As you accept yourself where you are with a growing sense of ease and rest, you will become aware of what your life is really like. The energy you spent being down on yourself is used instead for a kind of survey. What change would make life better, more satisfying? Are your relationships shallow? Does your family enjoy you? Do you long for a deeper communion with God and God's people?

There may be no way to change the ways other people have robbed you of opportunities or blocked you—the cruel abandonment, the bitter divorce, the heartless policies of companies you or someone in the family has worked for, the loss of finances. There is reality in all this,

but even with due regard to the past, isn't your overwhelming hunger now for the best possible relationships
with the people who mean most to you?

The awareness that comes with acceptance can reveal
how people see each of us, especially those we love. Do we
arouse impatience? Do we add our opinions to every conversation? Do we listen only to find a slice of silence so we
can jump into a conversation without down-right inter-
rupting? Do we, in fact, interrupt? Do we disapprove of
the way our grandchildren are handled and let it be
known, one way or another? That's the kind of thing that
needs changing if our relationships are to be rewarding
for ourselves and others. We do have lots of accumulated
experience and wisdom, but it's of no value unless we stop
to use it for a deeper awareness of how we behave. When
we accept the truth of what we see in ourselves, change
can come.

The biggest boost while you work with what you have is
God's presence inside you, hearing Jesus say, "Abide in me
as I abide in you." Using Jesus' words, "Blessed are the
poor in spirit," Henri Nouwen suggests that we all have a
place of poverty in our lives, a lack, an area in which we
feel thin and empty—that is our poverty, our poorness,
and it is there that we can find God's presence.[1] It may be
loneliness, it may be a lack of appreciation by family, it
may be a damaged relationship, but whatever it is, God is
most certainly there. How about that for a place to take a
deep breath, to relax a little, to let in some fresh air as you
work with what you've got?

Inner change is not easy. In Scrabble one moves the tiles
around on the little shelf—sometimes a new word is
revealed, sometimes not. Reshuffling your inner tiles
involves your mysterious inner world and it's a process
you can't always put a finger on. It's no wonder we hope
that something will happen outside ourselves to solve our

problems! You have a choice here: which discomfort shall you live with? Shall you live while your families react negatively to your behaviors and attitudes, or take an honest look at what has been causing uncomfortable relationships? Is it better to live with loneliness, a deep and conscious need for attention, with sharp-elbowing ways, with selfishness, or to face the discomfort that comes with having to change?

In his helpful article "Learning Jesus," Luke Timothy Johnson says "*Learning* demands *suffering* (italics in original) because it is painful to open the mind and the heart to new truth."[2] He goes on to explain that pain happens when we are shaken out of old habits, when we go *tilt* as we learn a new way to relate to someone, when we are caught off balance as change stares us in the face. My own growth made strides years ago as I began to learn the habit of a gentle acceptance of myself where I found myself then, and began to rethink and reshuffle my inner world so that my relationships with others would be more rewarding. There are still uncomfortable times of "one step forward and two steps back," but they are new steps—old backward ones are fading out behind me. It is a process that goes on. Acceptance releases the energy to change. This may take what time we have left, but it is rewarding and well worth the effort.

One rather humorous note, if one can see it, is that sometimes when we have changed no one seems to notice. People around us, especially our families, are used to our habits of behavior, don't expect change, and may not see it for a while. We've stopped jumping into conversations, we've stopped somewhat endless chatter, we no longer offer our firm opinions on any given subject, we've managed to curtail our tendency to interfere with the discipline of our grandchildren, we've managed to back off in general, but the appreciation doesn't come. Where's the pat on the back, the light of recognition in the eyes of our beholders, the "Well done, Mom!"? Doesn't seem to be there? That's okay. God is perfectly aware, and after all, the correction of unwelcome behavior has its own reward: you've accomplished something genuinely good. The best part is that our relationships will be easier, warmer, and that was the motivation that got us started. It was a hunger for more rewarding relationships with our loved ones that urged us on.

We've approached life like a game of Scrabble, taking a realistic look at what we have to play with, where we've come from with all we've experienced, and what we have now. We're conscious of what our grandchildren have been given in their life-game, and seek to relate to them in ways that will help. We use our own life-tiles to make relationships more rewarding.

Notes

1. Henri Nouwen, *Bread for the Journey* (San Francisco: Harper, 1997), Meditation for August 18.

2. Luke Timothy Johnson, "Learning Jesus," *The Christian Century,* 2 December 1998, 1143.

Nine

LITTLE LEAGUE AND BEYOND

(Being a Spectator)

The New Game

One morning I watched C. J.'s Seal Beach Kids Baseball game. The next day I was in the stands for Leslie's Girls' Summer Softball, and the following evening I took in Ian's high school varsity contest. I was a fully involved spectator.

I am also fully aware of the passage of time and some memories are indelible. It seems only yesterday that C. J. was three. Completely waterproofed, he's playing in puddles on the pier after a rain to the delight of older folks and the envy of young men. Now he's playing ball seriously enough to have a coach (his dad), an assistant coach, and real umpires.

I can still picture Leslie straddling the railing of our stairs—a favorite perch for several years on summer vacations with us. Commenting about Leslie on the occasion of her seventh-grade confirmation in the church, a former Sunday School teacher, looking back, said, "She's supposed to be in second grade." And now she's old enough to play second base, do child care on her own, and in happy ways is swiftly becoming a young woman.

When Ian was small he lived not far from a major highway spanned by an overpass. On a humid afternoon there he'd stand at the rail of the overpass on the lookout for the next semi barreling down the road. Sweat pouring down, he'd pump his arm while rig after rig acknowledged him with a blast of horn. Then he was three; now he's playing varsity ball, and has become an umpire himself.

The passage of time was reinforced when Maddie curiously stroked my wrinkled neck, and when Deanna said, "You're old, Grammie." Once I referred to her mom as a lovely lady and she said, "She's not a lady, she's a girl. Ladies are old, like you." Victor, one of my surrogate grands, asked me recently, "How old are you, Grandma?" When I said "Seventy-three," he said "Wow!" Most of the time I don't feel old, but the reality of things like wrinkles (a legacy from the days before sunblock) keep me alert to aging. I have a cousin who has turned 103—she's old. The seventies seem quite young.

Grandma Her Self

No one wants to lose her faculties, mental or physical, and no one needs to be told that with age there will be problems. Chip Andrus, in his song "Eighty-Seven Years," is taking his elderly grandmother in a Ryder van to a nursing home: he is reflecting on her wish to give away her possessions, to be content with a comfortable nightgown, and to hide her distaste for the whole thing.[1] Although aware of aging, just now I cannot worry much about a possible prolonged physical disability or Alzheimer's, even when I entertain some aches and discover the phone in the refrigerator. I'm busy living now, a great deal of which is being a grandma.

The spectator role will be increasingly activated. We want to be as mature as possible as we face the coming years, so it is important to consider the strategy for watching the game on the field from the stands. Now on occasion we are spectators at a ball game; down the road we will be permanent spectators, lacking strength to play games and physically on the sidelines. How does one watch the game of life well? Can we play the role of spectator graciously? Will people enjoy being in our presence even when we're physically confined?

When we're in the stands at a ball game we see and hear a variety of responses from the spectators. Some people cheer the players, some yell at the umpire, some are angry with the coach, some pay relatively little attention to the game but enjoy visiting with each other, some are just grumpy about the way the game is going, some are happy their team is winning, seldom does anyone put down the players on either team. What kind of spectator will you be in your grandmother sideline days?

The previous chapter suggests a process for becoming aware of who we really are, of careful and accepting listening to ourselves. The sooner you think about this the better you'll be prepared to be a spectator in the stands, for the quieter time coming. Acceptance allows awareness to come. When awareness shows us something negative, we keep practicing acceptance. I find it helpful to realize that this process toward inward maturity goes on both consciously and unconsciously once we have adopted this way of thinking and being. It is through accepting ourselves and becoming self-aware that change and growth go on. As this happens there is no need to be grumpy or angry at the people still out there on the field, the people we are with day by day; we may not be in control of events, but we are in control of ourselves.

I am writing as a single woman, a widow. It might seem a simpler process now for me, this way of acceptance and awareness, than for someone currently caring for a husband who is ill, or who has been bereft very recently, or who has responsibilities I haven't addressed. But the beauty of this process for growth is that it works for anyone at any age under any circumstances.

We get a boost in the direction of being gracious spectators when we're around our families and friends if we pay attention to what we say and how we act. Certainly we do not always want to be self-conscious, but it needs restating: if we become aware that our attitudes or behaviors are getting negative reactions from the people who are closest to us, we have a clear indication of what needs to be different if we're to be welcome.

An older woman became aware that her constant running chatter annoyed those closest to her and began to monitor her tongue. Another grandma became aware of her unpleasant habitual negative comments and began to put a more positive spin on events of the day. One grandma was guilty of a well-meant but heavy-handed spirituality; she knew her Bible and was quick to quote verses as advice on many and various occasions. She often gave answers when no one was asking questions. This kind of "spiritualizing" was an effort to impress and control, and while the offender may have been unconscious of her motives, the distancing effect was the same; people try to avoid a sermon no matter how simply or sweetly given.

God is capable of speaking to our loved ones without the nagging use of our voices. Giving up control of others (unless we are momentarily in charge) is perhaps the hallmark of a wise grandma.

We become aware of our limitations around the grandchildren in very practical ways. I chased Steven up a tall ladder at a park when he was only one and a half, and reflected later that I can't do that any more—I would need another adult in attendance at parks for ladders and slides. In the presence of grandchildren we tend to be less conscious of our behavior, to let our attitudes and tongues loose—and we demonstrate who we really are. I felt impatience with Madison because I had an unwelcome doctor's appointment on the immediate horizon; I was reminded that it is good to trace our feelings to their real cause. It is so easy to displace anger (or one of its smaller offspring: impatience, frustration, annoyance) onto children. Children do not upset us, they merely provide the occasion to activate what's already going on inside.

Sometimes these lessons from grandchildren come home to us only on reflection, later, when we're alone. This summer I told Leslie how very much we had appreciated her steady hands-on friendship with her little, so-much-younger cousins. She smiled and simply said, "Thank you." Later I reflected how gracious she was, no passing it off as if it were unimportant, no hint of "It really wasn't much." I used it as a lesson to myself to accept a compliment and not to ignore it as inconsequential or undeserved.

Like sitting with friends in the stands, I have four partner grandmothers. Each one has had years of experience in the school of life. Among these peers of mine, I'm the only one called Grandma; there are two Nanas, an Oma, and an Abuelita. Another has gone into God's real presence—she was called Grandmother, a dear friend with whom I had a great deal in common, both of us pastors' wives with five children. She was the first of my peers to go and her earthly death brought me genuine sorrow.

Two of these women live across the country and Guatemala is home for another. We are all very different but alike in so many ways. When Abuelita visits us from Guatemala we can only use the language of the heart, and one day as we were driving away from a market my daughter-in-law, our translator, was with us. We passed a man who was bald except for a long pony tail and we each commented on it, at the same time, in our respective languages. It was too funny, but it was also curiously poignant. When we part after a visit I know enough Spanish to recognize a blessing when I hear one.

Christmas comes more than once a year from one Nana who loads up a big box with well-chosen clothes and toys for grandchildren. I am hoping for an extended opportunity to visit with Oma, because she lived as a teenager in the Netherlands through the years of the Nazi occupation. I could be envious of the proximity of the other Nana to family, but am profoundly grateful for her caring ways and frequent care of the little ones. (Perhaps this is the place to wonder if "baby-sit" isn't an oxymoron. I stand for all grandmas who do child care and cannot remember having "sat," nor will ever merely "sit"—until the stands have claimed me.)

If competition should exist between you and another family grandmother, it's like sitting in the stands with the opposition at a game—uncomfortable and not to be desired. Personal rivalries use up energy that could be spent to cheer the players on. Overcoming these may take time, but God can guide you into small but significant overtures in this direction, and it may be up to you.

Does it need to be said that there's no place for rivalry between grandmothers and parents? When tears come from a little one after a fall, or weariness at the end of a long day of grandma, I have often heard, "I want my Mommy," or "When's Daddy coming?" A few weeks ago I was taking care of our six-year-old while his folks went to a movie. Into the evening he flatly stated: "I want my Mom." These small hopes sound good to me. Where would I be if these children didn't prefer their parents? Saddled with an enormous problem! When misunderstandings exist between grandmas and grown children, time alone doesn't heal. Love takes the initiative, some gentle effort on someone's part who is willing to back down and to bring about communication.

All grandmas have an enormous storehouse of memories, and memories can crowd into our consciousness as we head into the stands. What role do they play? Some memories nourish and lend energy, others diminish and draw us back where it does not help to go. When they are painful, I cannot think of anything quite so practical as giving them to God in a conversation with the One who already knows what's in that storehouse. Speaking to another person whom you trust comes next—speaking bad memories aloud lets you hear them with your own ears and gets them out in front of you where they lose some of their power. There may be a further activity to undertake—do you need to forgive or be forgiven?[2] Another useful tool when bad memories persist is immediately to fasten your mind on something else; reliving painful memories can become a habit that feeds on itself, a habit that can be broken with a persistent effort to shift thinking to something pleasant.

Particularly poignant or precious memories can take on a life of their own, and then care can be taken not to let them consume the present. Until we give way to the stands full-time we are not living to remember. We want to create new memories, not to let old ones consume us no matter how cherished.

Even when we can no longer get about physically we can be active mentally and spiritually. What kind of activity? Can we use the phone? Can we write notes? Can we pray? Some women confined in retirement homes pray on the phone, and people who need and value prayer have made good use of these prayer-people. Our prayers can influence how the game on the field plays out, and can bear eternal fruit.

Common sense can enter into our prayers. One woman told me about her prayer over a long period of time for the health of a certain person. She wondered: had she prayed hard enough to keep him alive but not hard enough to get him well? The reality is that only God knows the outcome of our praying and we aren't the ones with the keys of heaven and hell! I always enjoy praying early when I'm visiting in the Eastern Standard Time zone because I'm three hours ahead and the west coast families aren't even awake; I'm thinking that my prayers will be even more effective while they are still asleep. The reality is, however, that God is outside of time—there is no past or future with God but one eternal Now. Yesterday's prayers are as fresh as today's. The teenage daughter of friends had a peck of problems and I felt constrained to pray for her most ardently, off and on, for several days. Then I didn't, and when I remembered, guilt came. I recalled the time factor, and realized God was still hearing the old prayers. There are lovely references in Revelation to our prayers rising from golden bowls as incense before God's throne, new and old prayers always rising. (Revelation 5:8, 8:3–4)

Our activity as spectators is always to enter into the spirit of the game. Whether we are active onlookers around our families or passive participants from a distance, we want so much for the game to go well. A friend's two sons played football, and before each game she'd pray: "Let both sides do their best, and let there be no injuries." (Football players do need special prayers!) That small prayer is a useful pattern. We want everyone to do his or her best in our families, and we do not want injuries—accidents, illness, emotional strain, economic difficulties, work-related tensions, or anything else we can think of as we pray. We want perfection for these loved ones, but we know that we all learn from challenges, mistakes, and setbacks. Certainly there is gain without pain, but God is able to transform pain and show us possibilities for growth and renewal. When our children or their families suffer we suffer with them. God suffers with them.

A look at your own life and how the hours of your day tend to go will tell you the best time to spend with God, lifting each family, each individual in each family, for the blessing God alone can give. Countless people find early morning the best time, but each person has to find the time best for her. "Early Morning" is not the Eleventh Commandment. When we keep a definite time of more extended prayer it's easier to pray frequently throughout the rest of the day—or the night, if it's sleepless.

It may be that our spectator days will be our most important days of grandmothering. Because prayer is so important, the spectator days may be even more valuable to our families and to God than when we were active. Our active days can be a preparation for the slow ones to come.

Notes

1. Chip Andrus, "Let It Rain Down," Soul Highway Productions, CD.

2. Helpful books about forgiveness include David Augsburger, *Caring Enough to Forgive; Caring Enough Not to Forgive* (Ventura, Calif.: Regal Books, 1981); Louis Smedes, *Forgive and Forget* (New York: Pocket Books, 1990).

Ten

GOD'S GAME PLAN

(Being Part of the Ultimate Game)

The New Game Goes On

Today I had my picture taken for our church directory, chose one for my children, and agreed to have it "touched up." The salesman brought the touch-up menu to the computer screen and said, "Let's see what we want done," looked at my picture, and muttered, "Everything."

Not long ago, being invited on the spur of the moment to go somewhere I said, "I look pretty awful," and my grandson said, with the uncritical love he has for me, "You look like you always look, Grandma."

Well. So much for the outward appearance. The good

news is that as we grow older and our bodies are noticeably wearing out, as we are approaching the full-time spectator role, God is ever more interested in our *being* than our *doing.* God is more interested in what's going on inside than outside, yet it is the lack or loss of physical energy that most concerns us and threatens our peace. We tend to be more conscious of our inability to do things than of any emptiness or want inside.

The Bible very directly addresses our inner, spiritual journey as we age. In his letter to the Christians at Corinth, Paul wrote: "Even though our outer nature is wasting away, our inner nature is being renewed day by day" (2 Corinthians 4:16b). Eugene Peterson in *The Message* puts that verse this way: "Even though on the outside it often looks like things are falling apart on us, on the inside, where God is making new life, not a day goes by without his unfolding grace."[1]

"Wasting away" and "falling apart" are both strong phrases, but that's what is happening; it has been gradually happening through our adult years without our being quite so aware. Paul expands on this physical problem and the renewal of our inner world. He says:

> For this slight momentary affliction is preparing us for an eternal weight of glory beyond all measure, because we look not at what can be seen but at what cannot be seen; for what can be seen is temporary, but what cannot be seen is eternal. (2 Corinthians 4:17–18)

It is never too late to take advantage of the hope that positive change can happen within us while we are here on earth and that something far better is ahead of us. God's game plan was revealed in the initiative God took when Jesus was sent to show us who God is. When we hear Jesus speak and see Jesus in action we know what God says and what God does.[2]

God's Game Plan

We Christians base our faith on external historical events: Jesus of Nazareth lived an astonishing life, was crucified, died, and came back from the dead before returning to heaven. We are promised that he will come again to redeem all history and the whole cosmos, to make right what has gone wrong.

We are invited to become part of this big picture. Jesus invites us to himself, we who often fit his description of people in need: "Come to me, all you that are weary and are carrying heavy burdens, and I will give you rest" (Matthew 11:28). Jesus says, particularly to Christians who are lukewarm, "Listen! I am standing at the door, knocking; if you hear my voice and open the door, I will come in to you and eat with you, and you with me," a gracious invitation—for grandmas an increasingly more satisfying way to win life's big game (Revelation 3:20).

It is true for most of us that no matter how busy or tired or worn or sick we are, there are lucid moments during which we can speak to God even if we have never done so or if we haven't done so for a long time. If our minds go, if we can no longer consciously call on God, then God is still our God, God is still to be trusted.

God *always* meets us and sustains us where we are. Any faint breath of interest on our part, any brief signal to God that we want attention and are interested in connecting is sufficient to begin to renew or embrace a relationship with God. A friendship with God has many qualities of a human friendship—our awareness of it can ebb and flow, but unlike human friends who can be there for us only from time to time, God is steadily present.

There are skeptics, doubters, unbelievers. The bald truth seems to be that the world is wearing out even faster than we are—where is God, anyway? A woman whom I don't know well, so I do not know her faith story, had watched her mother deteriorate for some years, becoming increasingly frail yet stubbornly attached to life. She said to me, "God!! Even I could think of a better plan than this." To dismiss God because the world is full of pain and questions is to turn away from the only possible answer; it is, as David Alan Hubbard once said, "to pull the ceiling down on our heads."[3]

Aging can push grandfathers and grandmothers in God's direction or it can increasingly alienate us from God. Aging, however, when we are most conscious of being human, can bring us closest to Jesus who was always aware of his humanity and of God working in and through his human frailty.

As we read the Gospels we find Jesus always responding to those who were open. A woman fought the crowd to touch his garment and Jesus stopped to heal her and then to bless her; the children came to him and he honored them; Bartimaeus hollered from the roadside and Jesus stopped to meet his need; friends brought their sick companion to Jesus and he seemed to think nothing of the hole they made in the roof. Jesus demonstrated his cultural pluralism: he entered into intimate dialogue with a Samaritan woman, went to the home of a Roman centurion, healed the daughter of a Syro-Phoenician. Because of what Jesus showed us we know that God can be depended on to meet us whoever we are, wherever we are, at any minute in any twenty-four hours.

Our society has tried to hide death from us, but hushed tones, handsome caskets, clever embalming, and beautifully-lawned mortuaries do not work, and we are fearful. We are afraid of dying and of death—both are unknowns, and the unknown has its terrors.[4] In the face of the unknown, Jesus invites us to release our fears and to trust him in death as in life, to exchange fear for hope. Before he left his friends he said to them: "In my Father's house there are many dwelling places. If it were not so, would I have told you that I go to prepare a place for you?" (John 14:2) God's game plan is the ultimate plan because it includes eternity. Heaven is our destination; we can count on a place to go where we will be at home with God.

In the Celtic Christian view, death is a kind of grace that comes to us on our journey from earth; even a slow dying is a movement toward fulfillment in God. Death is "not a movement away from life but a grace through which we may move closer to life's source."[5] The very experiences of daily life prepare us for our death—the dying of the moments we have just lived, the dying of each day, the dying of seasons.

My grandson Matthew is one year old, too little for games, but on visits when he was younger I've helped with him and occasionally prevailed on his parents to let me take care of him at night. After a squawk or two while the bottle heated he would find comfort as I held him, and he was satisfied. Is it too much to suggest that a parent or grandparent's care of one who is too little to do anything for himself is a picture of God with us? God holds us through the gray time, through what to us seems the night.

This ultimate game is one that we all play. That God is in it, regardless of its brevity or length, its lack of suffering or awful pain, is a fact. God invites us to the habit of daily releasing our own fears. Grandmas with grandchildren in mind have enough to occupy us without letting fear get in the way. We can invite our grandchildren to release these fears and to learn to trust God. In our acceptance of them where they are we can be models of the love of Christ. We can also learn from children—they are quite ready to believe that we go to God when we die.

Pray that each of us will learn graces while we live that

will allow great grace at the end; this kind of prayer, prayer for each other on this journey, reflects the picture of ourselves as the body of Christ. You and I as grandmas are in this together. It is an adventure, and when we cannot clearly see the road ahead we know that God is with us on it. This road has been traveled by countless grandmothers and grandfathers before us—we are part of a great company.

Notes

1. Eugene H. Peterson, *The Message: The New Testament in Contemporary Language* (Colorado Springs: NavPress, 1994), 374.

2. A practical way to expand this insight is to study the life of Jesus as we find it in the Gospels: Matthew, Mark, Luke, and John. These are available on tape as well as in print. Be sure to choose a translation that uses the language you speak and hear every day.

3. From an adult Sunday School class at Lake Avenue Congregational Church in Pasadena, California, sometime in the 1960s.

4. The September/October 2000 issue of *Modern Maturity* magazine, in an unnumbered pull-out section "Start the Conversation: The *Modern Maturity* Guide to End-of-Life Care," addresses many financial and other practical aspects of the dying process. The PBS mini-series "On Our Own Terms: Moyers on Dying" may be ordered from your local PBS station or from Video Finders at 1-800-343-4727.

5. J. Philip Newell, *One Foot in Eden: A Celtic View of the Stages of Life* (Mahwah, N. J.: Paulist Press, 1999), 84.